Help!
There'll be 8 of us for dinner...
and I don't know much about cooking...

© 2007 Rebo International
This publication: © 2007 Rebo Productions b.v., Lisse

www.rebo-publishers.com
info@rebo-publishers.com

Text: Nicole Seeman
Photography: Raphaële Vidaling
Design: Claire Guigal
Original title: Au secours! on va être 8 à dîner et je ne sais pas trop cuisiner – 18 menus
à thème inratables même par les débutants
© 2006 Copyright SA, 12, Villa de Loucine, 75014, Paris, France
Translation: First Edition Ltd, Cambridge, UK
Editing: Sarah Dunham, Erin Slattery

ISBN: 978-90-366-2279-0

Help!
There'll be 8 of us for dinner …

And I don't know much about cooking …

18 themed menus that even a
beginner can't screw up

Text: Nicole Seeman
Photographs: Raphaële Vidaling

REBO
PUBLISHERS

Contents

Introduction

Why have a dinner party at home? After all, there are a lot of very nice restaurants around where you can eat very well, where all you have to do is put your feet under the table, where somebody else does the washing up, and where you will be greeted with a broad smile.

The pleasure of entertaining friends or family at home is a different pleasure, one that does not relate solely to the dining table. In the first place, it is an act of generosity which implies that you have devoted time to your guests. Secondly, it is a way of welcoming people to your home, of sharing intimacy. And above all, there is nothing quite like the end-of-evening atmosphere, with everyone slouched back on the sofa putting the world to rights. Discover the pleasure of giving pleasure by cooking...

In this book you will find...

- Lots of recipes to give you confidence when organizing dinner parties
    - planned for 8 people
    (without making you spend three days in the kitchen);
    - arranged by theme
    (but, obviously, you are free to mix and match them as you see fit);
    - fairly simple, in fact, foolproof
    (well, nobody's perfect);
    - that will cause a minor sensation
    (people can see that you have gone to some trouble);
    - with clearly written instructions
    (we don't all have to be bilingual in "master chef");
    - without too many complicated ingredients to track down.
- For each dinner, there are tips on how to get organized and how to prepare everything without stress.

The secrets behind making the most of your own dinner party

What makes for a successful dinner party is a cheerful and relaxed atmosphere. What goes on the plate is part, but not all of it. Your friends will gain more pleasure from having your company during the evening while eating very simple dishes than from tasting complex culinary feats that require you to spend the evening in the kitchen. If that is not the case, then they are not really friends! If you are too stressed out by your "culinary performance," you will be able to think of nothing else. Your mood will be in danger of veering from rosy to black, for fear that the meat will be overcooked or the vegetables soggy. Let's face it, it's just not worth it. There's also the danger of putting this pressure onto your guests, who will be so preoccupied with praising your dishes to the skies that there will be no other conversation at the table.

This dinner party has to be an enjoyable time for you too. Whatever happens, no matter how long you have spent slaving over a hot stove, your dishes will be gobbled up just as quickly. Tell yourself that the best compliment anyone can make you is not necessarily spoken, but rather that your guests ask for a second helping and that your dishes return to the kitchen empty.

A few thoughts to take the pressure off you:

· you are not in front of a panel of judges nor are you on trial;
· cooking is an ephemeral creation, so treat it as such;
· your friends like you and will continue to like you whatever you serve them.

What you can get your guests to do

Let's be clear about one thing: unless you live in a castle, having eight people in your kitchen is definitely too much. And there again, if you do live in a castle, it will be your servants who do the cooking—you won't even know where to find the kitchen. So, if you live in an ordinary, average house, the kitchen will have of necessity to be your domain. You can if you desire appoint an assistant. Choose either the most competent of your friends or the one who has made the most genuine offer to help. You can delegate tasks, rather like your parents did with you when you were little. Your guests can lay the table, help you serve the meal, and clear the plates afterward. As for the pile of dirty dishes, that is the preserve of extremely good friends, those who you want to share a post-mortem of the evening with questions such as:

· « "Do you think s/he likes me? Do you think they will call me again?"
· « "Aunt Martha, she can't really hold her liquor any more. Did you notice that she…"
· « "Be honest, just between ourselves, do you think the meat was slightly over-done; and the beans, were they cooked enough?"
· « "Don't you agree that Fred needs to update his style? He really must stop plastering his hair down with hair cream. Quite frankly, with it like that he looks like a playboy making a come-back…"

What to do when you haven't got time to make the entire meal

You sent your invites out a fortnight ago; your shopping and cooking plan is timed to perfection. Disaster strikes! Your boss calls a last-minute meeting, the train is stuck in a tunnel, your car just won't start… You are not a magician:

your potatoes won't peel themselves, your roast won't leap into the oven of its own accord.

Tip Number One: Find out in advance who makes the best food in your district.

Tip Number Two: Know which supermarkets are open late.

Tip Number Three: Always have to hand, next to the number for the police and the fire brigade, the number of a few good home delivery firms. After all, nobody will complain about good food, even if it wasn't you who picked the tomatoes, kneaded the dough, or killed the pig. What is important when you have not cooked the meal yourself is to take care over presentation. If you are dishing up a bought or delivered meal, serve it on pretty plates.

What you can serve without cooking it yourself:

As an appetizer:

· spreads: taramasalata, hummus, or eggplant caviar, with warm blinis or pitas;

· good cold cuts: a selection of sliced sausage and pâtés, for example prosciutto wrapped around bread sticks;

· preserved vegetables that you can find in Italian delis: sun-dried tomatoes, marinated eggplant and zucchini...

For the main course:

If you really can't make it yourself, have it delivered. Again, in that case, take the trouble to serve it on your own plates, just to go some way toward creating the illusion. That said, however, unless your guests are extremely unacquainted with the culinary arts, don't try to pass these dishes off as your own homemade. There are also some decent frozen meals around, although it is best to try them and test them beforehand as the lovely picture on the package is unfortunately no guarantee of quality.

For dessert:

Not really a secret, either you have a good bakery and everything is easy, or you buy a selection of quality ice creams and serve them in dishes or glasses with little pieces of meringue or crumbled cookies...

18 themed menus

The "Here's one I made earlier" dinner

or

how to be cool about entertaining when you get back from work at 8 P.M.

Carrot and ginger soup

Shredded southern chicken

Sumptuous chocolate and apricot cake

It's not necessary to spell out the appeal of these sort of recipes. Your friends arrive, you get back from work, and everything is ready. No stress, no race against the clock: you can welcome your guests with a smile.

"You must give me the recipes!" Virgil, who doesn't waste any time

Organization

Nothing special, as everything is prepared the evening before. Though, if you prefer, you can cook the rice at the last moment as it doesn't take long.

Other recipes in this book that can be prepared the evening before

Appetizers:
- Tomato and red pepper soup with cheese and herb chips (p. 80)
- Terrine of leeks with French dressing (p. 88)
- Homemade taramasalata with pink peppercorns (p. 128)
- Chicken liver mousse with raisins (p. 144)

"All this and you just got back from work a half hour ago?" Stephanie fooled by her host

Main courses:
- Cream of lentil soup with diced foie gras (p. 82)
- Meat and potato pie (p. 90)

Desserts:
- Green apple mousse (p. 28)
- Pears poached in wine, star anise, and crème de cassis (p. 36)
- Chocolate and ginger soup with litchis (p. 84)

Carrot and ginger soup

Ingredients

• 2 onions
• 4 tbsp olive oil
• 2 1/4 lb (1 kg) carrots
• 2 potatoes
• 3/4 inch (2 cm) fresh gingerroot or 2 tbsp ground ginger
• 6 cups (1.5 liters) water
• 2 slices country bread
• 8 sprigs cilantro
• 1 tbsp curry powder

Equipment

• 1 large saucepan or 1 heatproof casserole dish with a lid
• 1 potato peeler
• 1 skillet
• 1 electric beater
• paper towels

How long it will take

30 minutes preparation time
+ 40 minutes cooking time

Method

Peel the onions by removing the dried skin. Cut them in half lengthwise, then lay them flat side down and slice finely. In a large saucepan, heat 2 tablespoons olive oil over a moderate heat. Add the onion slices and cook for 10 minutes. They should become transparent without browning, if necessary lower the heat. While the onions are cooking, peel the carrots and potatoes. Cut the carrots into roughly 1/2 inch (1 cm) thick slices and dice the potatoes. If you are using fresh gingerroot, peel it and cut into slices. After 10 minutes, add the diced potatoes, carrots, ginger (fresh or ground), and water to the pan. Cover, reduce the heat, and simmer for 30 minutes. Meanwhile, remove the crust from the country loaf slices and cut the bread into small cubes. Place a paper towel on a plate. Heat the skillet over a high heat. When it is hot, add the remaining 2 tablespoons of olive oil. When the oil is very hot, add the cubes of bread. Sauté, stirring frequently, until golden and crispy. Drain on the paper towel. When the vegetables are cooked, remove the pieces of fresh ginger, if used, and process the mixture in a blender until smooth. Allow the soup to cool, then put in a refrigerator. Store the croutons in an airtight container. When ready to serve, reheat the soup over a low heat. Wash and dry the cilantro leaves. Serve the soup in bowls or soup plates, sprinkled with the croutons, cilantro leaves, and curry powder.

Shredded southern chicken

Ingredients

- 4 onions
- 6 tbsp olive oil
- 8 chicken thighs
- 4 garlic cloves
- 2 oranges
- 1 lemon
- 1 bottle dry white wine (use an inexpensive wine, as it's for cooking)
- 2 large cans sliced mushrooms (about 3 cups/450g, drained)
- 1 large can peeled tomatoes (about 1 cup/450g, drained)
- 2 handfuls raisins
- 2 handfuls black olives (warn your guests if the olives are not pitted so that they don't break any teeth)
- 2 tbsp paprika
- 3 cups (600g) basmati rice
- A few strands of saffron to color the rice (optional)
- 2 tsp butter
- Salt and pepper

How long it will take
30 minutes preparation time
+ 2 1/2 hours cooking time

Equipment
- 1 large saucepan or 1 heatproof casserole with 1 lid
- 1 nonstick skillet
- 1 zester
or 1 potato peeler
- 1 large saucepan
- plastic wrap

Method
Peel the onions by removing the dried skin. Place them flat side down and cut into slices about 1/8 inch (3 mm) thick. Heat the casserole dish over a moderate heat. When it is hot, add 2 tablespoons olive oil and heat. Add the onion slices and cook for about 10 minutes until soft and transparent. Place the skillet over a high heat. When it is hot, add 2 tablespoons of olive oil. When the oil is very hot, add four chicken thighs. Cook for about

10 minutes, turning once, until they are golden. Transfer to a plate, set aside, and then repeat with the remaining chicken thighs. While the chicken is cooking, peel the garlic cloves by removing the skin and chopping finely. Using a zester or potato peeler, cut strips of orange zest, then cut them into fine shreds if necessary. Squeeze the lemon and the oranges. Place the chicken thighs on the onions. Add the white wine. Drain the canned mushrooms and tomatoes and add to the casserole, together with the garlic, raisins, olives, orange and lemon juice, half the orange zest strips, and the spices. Season with salt and pepper. Bring to a boil, then reduce the heat, and cover. While the chicken is cooking, cook the rice, following the instructions on the package, adding the saffron threads if you wish. Drain the rice, allow to cool, then transfer to a large bowl, cover with plastic wrap, and keep in the refrigerator. When the chicken is cooked, allow it to cool. While cooking, the flesh will have fallen away from the bone, together with the skin. Remove the bones and the skin from the casserole and discard. The remaining meat will be in shreds and small pieces. When it is cold, place in the refrigerator. The next day, the day of the dinner party, reheat the chicken over a low heat, uncovered. Gently reheat the rice with the butter in a saucepan or microwave.

Sumptuous chocolate and apricot cake

Ingredients

· 24 dried apricots
· 7 oz (200 g) bittersweet chocolate
· I cup (200g) lightly salted butter
· 3 eggs
· Generous I cup (250 g) sugar
· I/2 cup (50 g) flour
If the baking pans you intend to use are not nonstick:
· I tsp butter
· 2 tbsp sugar

Equipment

· I electric or hand beater
· I large cake pan or 8 small muffin pans (nonstick if possible)
· plastic wrap

How long it will take

30 minutes preparation time
+ 30 minutes cooking time

Method

Preheat the oven to 350 °F (180 °C). Cut 16 apricots into small dice—the remaining apricots will be used for decoration. Break the chocolate into small pieces. Melt the chocolate with the butter either in a saucepan over a very low heat or in a microwave oven at 30-second blasts (stirring gently between blasts). Stir, then pour the chocolate into a mixing bowl and allow to cool. Beat together the eggs and the sugar until the mixture is pale yellow and frothy. Pour over the melted chocolate and butter, beating well. Add the flour and beat again, then add the diced apricots, and combine. If your baking pans are not nonstick, grease them with butter using a paper towel, then add a little sugar, turning the pans upside down to remove any excess. Transfer the mixture to the muffin pans or to the large cake pan. Bake in the oven for 25 minutes. When cooked, remove from the oven and allow to rest for 20 minutes before turning out. Keep the cakes wrapped in plastic wrap. If you have used a large cake pan, cut the cake into eight pieces before serving. Decorate with the remaining dried apricots.

Ultra light dinner

or

dinner without the calorific consequences

Marinated shrimp with cilantro and watercress

Cod on a bed of tomatoes and zucchini

Green apple mousse

Ultra light doesn't mean ultra bland, or ultra boring, or that your guests will still be hungry when they leave the table. All it means is not much butter, cream, or oil. Herbs and spices are there to tickle the taste buds. And after all, sometimes it is better not to need a five-hour siesta after a meal. And, of course, everyone has got friends who blanch at the idea of the calories they are going to consume when they are asked round for a meal. With this menu, they won't have to exclaim, "No sauce for me!" or, "Actually, I'm allergic to butter" etc., which does tend to put a damper on things. Here, everyone can enjoy themselves, without any complexes, stress, or guilt. Even your friends who are on a diet will come back.

"Speaking for myself, I feel ultra well!" Gerald, who has good reason to watch his weight

Organization

The evening before, you can…
· Make the bed of tomatoes and zucchini: just reheat it when ready to serve.
· Make the apple mousse, apart from the strips, cutting them on the day itself so that they don't turn brown.

A few hours before the meal, you can…
· Shell the shrimp, make the lime sauce, pour half of it over the shrimp, then put in the refrigerator.

"I agree, but a little cream doesn't do any harm either." Émilie, intractable gourmand

Just before your guests arrive, you can…
· Make up the shrimp with cilantro and watercress.
· Cook the cod fillets: all you have to do is put them in the oven.

Marinated shrimp with cilantro and watercress

Ingredients
- 3 limes
- 12 tbsp olive oil
- About 32 large shrimp, ready cooked (fresh or frozen)
- 4 cups (200 g) watercress leaves (or any other small-leafed salad, such as arugula, corn salad, baby spinach…)
- 8 sprigs cilantro

Equipment
- 1 lemon squeezer

How long it will take
- 20 minutes preparation time

Method
Squeeze two limes. Combine the juice with the olive oil. Carefully shell the shrimp using your fingers, removing first the head and the tail, then peeling off the body shell. Put the shelled shrimp in a mixing bowl, pour over half the lime sauce, and combine. Wash the watercress if necessary. Wash and dry the cilantro leaves. Combine the remaining sauce with the watercress leaves and spoon onto the plates. Place the shrimp on top of the watercress. Cut the remaining lime into thin slices and arrange on the plates as decoration. Sprinkle with the cilantro leaves.

Cod on a bed of tomatoes and zucchini

Ingredients
- 12 tomatoes
- 4 onions
- 4 zucchini
- 2 lemons
- 6 tbsp olive oil
- About 24 pitted olives
- 8 cod steaks
- 6 sprigs thyme (fresh if possible, otherwise dried)
- Salt and pepper

Equipment
- 1 lemon zester or 1 potato peeler
- 1 lemon squeezer
- 1 large saucepan or 1 heatproof casserole dish
- 1 large ovenproof dish (large enough to hold 8 cod steaks arranged side by side)

How long it will take
30 minutes preparation time
+ 30 minutes cooking time

Method
Preheat the oven to 350 °F (180 °C). Wash the tomatoes and cut each one into eight pieces. Peel the onions by removing the dried skin, then cut in half lengthwise. Place them flat side down and slice finely. Wash the zucchini, remove the ends, then cut in half lengthwise and cut into thin slices. If you have a zester, use it to remove the lemon zest. Otherwise, remove long strips of zest using a potato peeler and cut into fine shreds. Squeeze one of the lemons. In a large saucepan or casserole dish, heat 3 tablespoons of olive oil over a moderate heat. Add the onion slices and cook for 10 minutes until they are transparent but have not browned. If necessary, reduce the heat. After 10 minutes, add the tomato pieces, sliced zucchini, strips of lemon zest, olives, salt, and pepper. Cook for 20 minutes. While the vegetables are cooking, spread a tablespoon of olive oil over the base of the ovenproof dish. Sprinkle salt over both sides of the

cod steaks, then arrange in the dish. Combine the lemon juice with 2 tablespoons of olive oil and pour over the cod steaks. Arrange the thyme sprigs over the fish and bake in the oven for 10 minutes. Spoon the vegetables onto plates and top with the cod.

Green apple mousse

Ingredients

· 10 Granny Smith apples
· 4 cups (1 kg) light fromage blanc or Quark
· 1/2 cup (100 g) superfine sugar or 10 (0.035 oz/1 g) envelopes sugar substitute (for an even lighter version)
· 8 sheets of leaf gelatin (from gourmet and bakery supply stores)
· 1 cup (240 ml) water

Equipment

· 1 food processor with grater attachment or 1 hand grater (but it is rather more tedious)

How long it will take

30 minutes preparation time + at least 2 hours chilling time in the refrigerator

Method

Cut eight of the apples into quarters, remove the cores, and peel. Grate them into strands (as for carrots). Combine the cheese with the sugar or sugar substitute, then add the grated apples. Place the sheets of gelatin in a small saucepan together with the water.

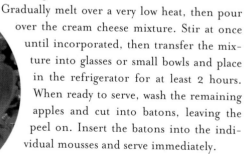

Gradually melt over a very low heat, then pour over the cream cheese mixture. Stir at once until incorporated, then transfer the mixture into glasses or small bowls and place in the refrigerator for at least 2 hours. When ready to serve, wash the remaining apples and cut into batons, leaving the peel on. Insert the batons into the individual mousses and serve immediately.

Cheap and chic dinner

or

how to keep the peace with your bank manager

Cream of mushroom soup with crispy ham

Roast pork with gingerbread cream sauce and apple

Pears poached in wine, star anise, and crème de cassis

You haven't won the lottery this month. What's more, you didn't win last month either. To put it bluntly, you're flat broke, you're on your uppers, you haven't got a dime. You imagine your bank manager is rolling his eyes at you in despair. But that is no reason not to have friends round: you just need to adapt your recipes to your slightly tightened means. "It's good because it's expensive" becomes "It's not a case of it not being good because it's not expensive." There are lots of tasty dishes you can rustle up without breaking the bank. All you need do is pay a little attention to presentation and you will have a dinner for eight that won't bring you to the poverty line, without your guests ever feeling that they've been offered prison rations.

Organization

The evening before, you can...
· Make the cream of mushroom soup without adding the cream (keep in the refrigerator overnight).
· Cook the potatoes and onions for the roast pork.
· Make the pears poached in wine.

"Asking friends for dinner without breaking the bank means you can entertain more often at home." Grégoire, whose heart is bigger than his budget

"My main memory is that I ate very well." Benoît, the perfect guest

"I had never tasted gingerbread sauce before, it's brill!" Hélène, another perfect guest

Cream of mushroom soup with crispy ham

Ingredients
- 4 1/2 lb (2 kg) cultivated mushrooms
- 4 garlic cloves
- 3 tbsp oil
- 4 cups (1 liter) water
- 2 bouillon cubes
- 4 slices jambon cru or prosciutto
- 8 sprigs chervil (or chives)
- 2 cups (500 ml) light cream
- Salt

Equipment
- 1 large heatproof casserole dish or 1 saucepan with 1 lid
- 1 skillet
- paper towels
- 1 blender

How long it will take
35 minutes preparation time
+ 45 minutes cooking time

Method
Wipe and dry the mushrooms. Remove the gritty stem bases, then slice coarsely. Peel the garlic cloves by removing the dry skin. Heat the casserole over a high heat. When hot, add 3 tablespoons of oil. When the oil is very hot, add the sliced mushrooms and peeled garlic cloves and fry for about 7 minutes until golden. Add the water and the bouillon cubes, bring to a boil, then reduce the heat, cover, and simmer for about 30 minutes. Meanwhile, finely dice the jambon cru or prosciutto. Place a paper towel on a plate. Heat the skillet over a high heat and sauté the pieces of ham until very crispy (35 minutes). Transfer them to the paper towel and leave to cool. Wash and dry the herbs. If using chervil, remove the leaves from the stalk; if using chives, snip them into small pieces. When the mushrooms are cooked, process them together with the liquid in a blender. Rinse out the casserole. Return the mixture to the casserole dish and heat over a low heat. Add three-quarters of the cream and stir. Check the sea-

soning, adding a little salt if necessary and a little water if the mixture is too thick. When it is heated through, serve in bowls with a swirl of cream, garnished with the herbs and the crispy ham squares.

Roast pork with gingerbread cream sauce and apple

Ingredients

· I pork joint weighing 3 1/2 lb (1.6 kg)
· 5 tbsp oil
· I cup (240 ml) water
· 2 onions
· 4 slices gingerbread
· 3 cups (750 ml) light cream
· I tbsp mustard
· 4 Golden Delicious apples
· 2 tsp butter
· Salt and pepper

Equipment

· I ovenproof dish
· I skillet
· I blender
· I potato peeler
· I saucepan
· I large knife to carve the roast

How long it will take

40 minutes preparation time
+ I hour cooking time

Method

Preheat the oven to 400 °F (200 °C). Place the pork joint in the ovenproof dish. Coat with 3 tablespoons of oil, season all over with salt and pepper, and pour the water into the dish. Roast the joint in the oven for 45 minutes, basting from time to time with the liquid in the dish. Peel and halve the onions, then place flat side down and cut into roughly 1/4 inch (0.5 cm) thick slices. Pour 2 tablespoons of oil into the skillet and heat over a moderate heat. When hot, add the onion slices and cook for 10–15 minutes, until they are transparent and have browned slightly. While the onions are cooking, process the gingerbread slices, cream, and mustard in a blender. When the onions are cooked, remove them from the skillet. Cut the apples into quarters, remove the cores, peel, and cut each quarter into four slices. Heat the skillet you used for the onions (there's no need to wash it out) over a high heat. When hot, melt the butter. When the butter has melted, add the apple pieces and cook for about 6–10 minutes until beautifully golden. At the end of the 45-minute cooking time, remove the joint from the oven. Arrange the apples and onions around the meat and return to the oven to cook for an additional 15 minutes. Meanwhile, heat the gingerbread sauce in a saucepan over a moderate heat until it is

thoroughly combined and very hot. Season to taste with salt and pepper. When ready, remove the dish from the oven and allow to rest for 10 minutes. Slice the roast pork and serve with the apple and onion garnish. Place the sauce on the table for people to help themselves.

Pears poached in wine, star anise, and crème de cassis

Ingredients

• 8 pears
• 1/2 lemon
• 1 bottle red wine (choose an inexpensive one)
• 1 3/4 cups (400 g) superfine sugar
• 8 whole star anise (you will find them in the spice aisle; if not, use powdered star anise or cinnamon and cloves)
• 6 tbsp crème de cassis liqueur

Equipment

• 1 potato peeler
• 1 lemon squeezer
• 1 large saucepan or heatproof casserole dish

How long it will take

20 minutes preparation time
    + 1 hour cooking
        time

Method

Cut the pears in half lengthwise. Using a knife, remove the stalk and the core, then peel the pears. Squeeze the lemon. In a saucepan, bring the wine, sugar, star anise, and lemon juice to a boil, then add the halved pears. Reduce the heat and simmer for 45 minutes, then remove the pears, and set aside. Retain about 2 cups (500 ml) of the wine sauce in the pan. Bring to a rolling boil and continue to boil until the sauce has reduced by half. The sauce should now be quite syrupy. Add the crème de cassis liqueur and cook for an additional 5 minutes. Place two pear halves on each plate and pour over the sauce. Decorate with star anise.

The whole family dinner

or

everyone makes…
what he likes…

Mini puff pastry pizzas

*Chicken burgers,
baked potatoes*

*Readymade sweet pas-
try tartlets*

Struggling to get everyone happily together around the table? In this menu, there are three dishes that are favorites with children, easy to eat and easy to make. Admittedly it's not haute cuisine, but more a way of avoiding having to produce two menus, a serious one for the adults and a fun one for the children. Sharing enjoyment at meal times is possible at any age: as long as you start early. And there again, just because you've grown up it doesn't mean you no longer like Nutella! Everyone can make up their meal as they like: pizza with or without ham, with or without olives, burgers with or without mayonnaise, potatoes with or without cream... And for dessert, both children and grown-ups can create their own tartlets, decorating them as they choose. Fun, games, and a healthy appetite guaranteed!

Organization

"For once, Joseph ate everything, his sister ate everything, and their dad ate everything. Wow!" Astrid, quite relaxed for once!

The evening before, you can...
· Bake the pastry.

A few hours before, you can...
· Bake the pizza bases with the tomato sauce.
· Prepare the pizza toppings.
· Bake the potatoes, reheating them at the last minute.
· Toast the buns for the burgers.
· Prepare, but not cook the burgers, and keep them in the refrigerator.
· Make the burger fillings.

"Yum-yum, it's great." Paul, aged 5, very happy

Mini puff pastry pizzas

Ingredients
- 2 rounds ready-rolled puff pastry
- 2 cups (500 g) tomato sauce
- 2 slices ham
- 2 slices prosciutto
- 4 mozzarella cheeses, each weighing about 9 oz (250 g)
- About 40 pitted olives
- Any other pizza toppings of your choice, such as marinated bell peppers, sliced mushrooms, anchovies…

Equipment
- 1 baking sheet

How long it will take
20 minutes preparation time
+ 40 minutes cooking time

Method
Preheat the oven to 350 °F (180 °C). Cut each of the two rounds of puff pastry into four pieces. Leave them on the packing paper, separating them slightly so that they do not stick when cooking. Place half the pieces on the baking sheet, spread with tomato sauce, and bake for 15 minutes. Remove from the oven and allow to cool. Repeat the process with the remaining pastry. Prepare the ingredients for the pizza toppings: dice the ham, prosciutto, and mozzarella, halve the olives, etc. When seated at the table, everyone makes up their pizza as they like. When ready to eat, heat the broiler and cook the pizzas as required until the cheese has melted (between 3 and 5 minutes).

Chicken burgers, baked potatoes

Ingredients

- 8 large potatoes
- 24 blades of chive
- 2 cups (500 ml) thick crème fraîche or sour cream
- 2 large tomatoes
- 4 scallions or 2 ordinary onions
- 8 hamburger buns
- 8 skinless chicken breasts
- 1 small carton plain yogurt
- 4 tbsp flour
- 4 tbsp oil
- Salt and pepper

Equipment

- aluminum foil
- baking sheet
- 1 toaster (optional)
- 1 blender
- 1 or 2 nonstick skillets

How long it will take

30 minutes preparation time + 1 hour cooking time

Method

Preheat the oven to 400 °F (200 °C). Wash but do not peel the potatoes. Wrap each potato in aluminum foil, place on a baking sheet, and bake for 1 hour. Meanwhile, wash and dry the chives. Using a knife or a pair of scissors, snip the chives into roughly 1/8 inch (3 mm) long pieces. Stir the chives into the crème fraîche or sour cream and season with salt and pepper. Place in the refrigerator. Wash, dry, and slice the tomatoes. Remove one layer of skin from the small onions, then slice the white parts only (or peel and slice the ordinary onions). If you desire, you can toast the hamburger buns. In a blender, quickly process the chicken breasts with the yogurt, salt, and pepper (the longer you blend, the stickier the chicken flesh will become). Coat your hands with the flour to prevent the mixture sticking and shape the chicken mixture into eight burgers. About 10 minutes before the end of the cooking time for the potatoes, heat the skillet(s) over a high heat. When hot, add half the oil, and heat. Place four burgers in each skillet (if you have only one skillet, you will have to cook them in two batches). Cook for 4 minutes, then turn using a spatula and cook for an additional 4 minutes. Remove the potatoes from the oven, leaving them in the aluminum foil. Serve all the ingredients together so that everyone can make their own burger as they like. The cream and chive dip is intended to go with the baked potatoes.

Readymade sweet pastry tartlets

Ingredients

• 2 rounds ready-rolled sweet short pastry (ready-rolled pastry is packed in paper that can be used as a backing while cooking)
• I jar Nutella or other hazelnut and chocolate spread
• Selection of fruit, such as bananas, grapes, strawberries, raspberries, etc.
• 8 tbsp thick crème fraîche or sour cream
• 4 tbsp superfine sugar

Equipment

• I baking sheet

How long it will take

20 minutes preparation time
+ 20 minutes cooking time

Method

Take the pastry out of the refrigerator (and the Nutella, if that's where you keep it, so that it will soften and be easier to spread). Preheat the oven to 400 °F (200 °C). Unroll the pastry and cut out circles using a small glass or bowl as a cutter. Take care not to tear the paper. Repeat the procedure with the second pastry round. Remove the excess pastry, leaving the pastry rounds on the packing paper. When the oven has reached the correct temperature, place half the pastry rounds together with the paper on the baking sheet and bake for IO minutes. Repeat with the remaining pastry. While it is cooking, wash the fruit, peeling and chopping it if necessary. Combine the crème fraîche or sour cream with the sugar. When ready, remove the pastry rounds from the oven and allow to cool. When everyone is ready for their dessert, they can make up their own little tartlets.

Dinner in less than an hour

or

how to entertain
like Speedy Gonzales

*Crostinis with moz-
zarella and peppers*

*Tuna in a tapenade
crust with Parmesan
pasta*

*Cream cheese with
maple syrup and pecan
nuts*

Yes, it really can be done! The secret of a fast feast, especially one for eight people, lies in assembly cooking. Not a very pretty phrase, but all it means is that rather than starting from scratch with all the basic ingredients, you just assemble things that others (food manufacturers, artisan producers, your mother…) have already made to transform them into "homemade" dishes. It's one step up from "all caterer" or "all supermarket."

Organization

Just before your guests arrive, you can…

- Make the crostinis; all you have to do is pop them in the oven.
- Cook the tuna steaks; all you have to do is pop them in an oven.
- Spoon the cream cheese into bowls with the pecan nuts. When ready to serve, drizzle with the maple syrup.

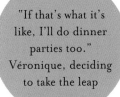

"If that's what it's like, I'll do dinner parties too."
Véronique, deciding to take the leap

"One hour, that's 60 minutes, in other words 3,600 seconds. If you put it that way, it actually seems quite a long time!"
Jérémy, good at math

"I don't believe it, it's just not possible! Really, less than an hour, for 8 people?"
Antoine, fooled guest

Crostinis with mozzarella and peppers

Ingredients
· 8 basil leaves
· 8 large slices country bread
· 4 mozzarella di bufala cheeses (mozzarella made from buffalo milk, which has a better flavor), otherwise ordinary cow's milk mozzarella cheese
· 2 jars, each about 10 oz (280 g), of bell peppers marinated in oil

Equipment
· 1 toaster (optional)
· 1 baking sheet

How long it will take
10 minutes preparation time
+ 5 minutes cooking time

Method

Heat the broiler. Wash and dry the basil leaves. Toast the bread in a toaster or on a baking sheet under the broiler (in which case you will have to turn them to toast both sides). Slice the mozzarella cheeses and cut the peppers into strips. Divide the mozzarella between the slices of toast and top with the peppers. Arrange the crostinis on a baking sheet and place under the broiler. Watch carefully. When the cheese is thoroughly melted (it will take about 3 minutes), remove from the broiler, garnish with the basil leaves, and serve.

Tuna in a tapenade crust with Parmesan pasta

Ingredients

- 2 tbsp salt for cooking the pasta
- 7 tbsp olive oil
- 8 tuna steaks, skin and bones removed
- 8 tbsp black tapenade (an olive spread)
- 1 lb 2 oz (500 g) pasta (penne, for example)
- 1/4 lb (100 g) Parmesan cheese, in a piece or grated
- 1 lemon
- 8 blades of chive (optional garnish)
- Salt and pepper

Equipment

- 1 large saucepan to cook the pasta
- 1 large ovenproof dish
- 1 potato peeler if making Parmesan shavings
- 1 sieve
- 1 lemon squeezer

How long it will take

10 minutes preparation time
+ 12 minutes cooking time

Method

Preheat the oven to 400 °F (200 °C). Put a large saucepan of water to boil and add 2 tablespoons of salt. Cover the base of the ovenproof dish with 3 table-spoons of olive oil and arrange the tuna steaks on top. Spread 1 tablespoon of tapenade on each tuna steak. When the water has come to a rolling boil, add the pasta, and cook for the time shown on the package. Bake the tuna for 10 min-utes. Meanwhile, use a potato peeler to make shavings from the block of Parmesan cheese. Squeeze the lemon. Wash and dry the chives and cut the blades

into three. When the pasta is cooked (taste a piece to check), drain and transfer to a serving dish, season with salt and pepper, and combine with 4 tablespoons of olive oil and the lemon juice. Remove the tuna from the oven. Garnish with the snipped chives. Serve the tuna with the pasta and Parmesan cheese alongside for people to serve themselves as they like.

Cream cheese with maple syrup and pecan nuts

Ingredients
· About 4 cups (1 kg) fromage blanc or mascarpone cheese
· 16 tbsp maple syrup (you can use honey instead)
· 24 pecan nuts (alternatively, use walnuts)

Equipment
None

How long it will take
10 minutes preparation time

Method
Strain the cheese if necessary and divide among the bowls. Pour 2 tablespoons of maple syrup over each bowl, but do not mix. Arrange the nuts over the cheese around the maple syrup. That's all, it's ready.

Finger buffet dinner

or

how to rediscover the sense of touch at the table

Vegetable and duck spring rolls, soy dipping sauce

Crispy pork spareribs, whole corn

Brioche club sand- wiches

Eating involves all five senses, but the one that we usually use least is touch (apart from when the food is already in our mouths). Here, we are going to use the hands in each stage of the dinner. The hands enable the mouth to anticipate the texture of the dish: soft, crispy, hot, firm…

Admittedly, you do run the risk of burning yourself as the butter from the corn runs over the chin, but what a joy it is to lick your fingers! It's a very effective way of relaxing around a rather cramped table of people.

However, for a finger buffet supper, don't lay on:

· meat or cheese fondue
· onion soup
· lobster
· very ripe Camembert cheese

"Not good for my manicure, but it's hysterical." Éléonore, who joins in the fun

Organization

"But look, I've got a place setting after all!" Jeanne, who didn't quite get the point

The evening before, you can…
· Make the vegetable rolls and the sauce.

A few hours before, you can…
· Sauté the brioche slices.
· Prepare the pork spareribs, ready to put them in the oven.
· Cook the corn ears, reheating them at the last minute.

"Spring rolls, you'd think we were in China…" Julien, who has a vivid imagination

Vegetable and duck spring rolls, soy dipping sauce

Ingredients

- 6 tbsp olive oil
- 2 tbsp soy sauce
- I tbsp nuoc-mam sauce (Asian sauce available from specialty Asian markets)
- I tbsp superfine sugar
- I bell pepper
- 2 carrots or I cup ready-grated carrot
- 24 slices cured duck breast
- 24 spring roll skins (approximately 6 inches/16 cm in diameter)
- I 1/2 cups (100 g) bean sprouts
- 4 tbsp sesame seeds

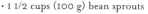

Equipment

- I grater if using whole carrots
- paper towels

How long it will take

45 minutes preparation time

Method

Combine the olive oil, soy sauce, nuoc-mam, and sugar, stirring well to dissolve the sugar. Wash and halve the bell pepper. Using a knife, remove the seeds and the white membranes. Cut the pepper into thin strips about 2 inches (5 cm) long. Peel and grate the carrots if necessary. Remove the fat from the duck breast if you do not like it. Pour some water into a shallow dish. Place one spring roll skin in the water and wait until it is very soft. Carefully take it out of the water, drain on a paper towel, and place on a plate. Place a slice of duck breast on top, together with some bean sprouts, strips of bell pepper, and grated carrot. Fold over two sides of the wrapper, then roll tightly around the ingredients to form a small roll. Sprinkle a few sesame seeds over the roll. Repeat for the remaining skins. Serve three spring rolls per person together with the dipping sauce in small bowls.

Crispy pork spareribs, whole corn

Ingredients

· 8 whole ears of corn
· Salt
· 4 1/2 lb (2 kg) pork spareribs
· 8 tbsp honey
· 8 tbsp soy sauce
· 8 knobs of butter

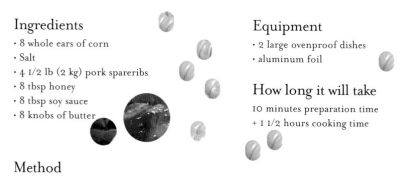

Equipment

· 2 large ovenproof dishes
· aluminum foil

How long it will take

10 minutes preparation time
+ 1 1/2 hours cooking time

Method

Preheat the oven to 400 °F (200° C). Place the corn in an ovenproof dish, sprinkle with salt, and bake for 40 minutes. While the corn is cooking, slice between every other bone of the pork spareribs. Place in a large ovenproof dish. Combine the honey with the soy sauce and pour over the meat pieces, turning to coat on both sides. When the ears of corn are cooked, remove them from the oven and cover with aluminum foil to keep them hot. There is no need to remove the leaves if they have them. Put the dish of spareribs in the oven. After 15 minutes, remove the dish from the oven, turn the spareribs over, and return them to the oven for an additional 15 minutes. Turn on the broiler and place the dish of spareribs under it. After 5 minutes, check to see if the ribs have caramelized nicely. If not, leave them under the broiler for a bit longer. Turn the spareribs again and leave them under the broiler for an additional 3 minutes, until they are nicely caramelized on the other side too. Remove the spareribs and return the corn to the oven to reheat for about 5 minutes. Pour the cooking juices over the meat. Everyone can melt a knob of butter on their corn ear.

Brioche club sandwiches

Ingredients

· 1/2 cup (100 g) butter
· 1/2 cup (100 g) superfine sugar
· 16 slices brioche
· 4 cups (800 g) chestnut puree
· 1 aerosol whipped cream

Equipment

· 1 large nonstick skillet

How long it will take

10 minutes preparation time
+ 20 minutes cooking time

Method

Over a moderate heat, melt a quarter of the butter in the skillet. When it has melted, add a quarter of the sugar and wait until it melts and begins to brown. Place four slices of brioche in the skillet, turning them when golden (after about 1 minute). Cook until the other side is golden. Add more butter and sugar and repeat the process until all the brioche slices are cooked. Spread the chestnut puree over eight brioche slices, top with the remaining slices, and cover with whipped cream.

Christmas dinner

"Merry Christmas, Merry Christmas" Françoise, who has had too much champagne

or
how to become a Father (or Mother) Christmas of the kitchen

Potato and smoked salmon mille-feuilles

Duck breasts with foie gras and morels

Chocolate and candied orange tart

And yes, like every year, Christmas is going to arrive with its trail of garlands, pine trees, and presents. Christmas is not usually the time for wild trips of culinary fancy. It is more a matter of preparing a meal based on traditional, festive foods that do not take too long to cook and are not too costly. What is important, and just as much so as the food, is to create a beautiful table setting that immediately tells your guests that this is not just any old day, nor is it just any old meal. Don't skimp on the red, the gold decorations, the candles. Down with good taste and sobriety. Don't worry if you don't have real silverware, crystal soufflé dishes, or embroidered linen table napkins. All you need to decorate the table are a few Christmas tree baubles stacked up in vases, paper napkins tied with pieces of tinsel, a profusion of candles, and some pine branches. In a nutshell, a few inexpensive accessories will make your table a place worthy of welcoming Father Christmas himself.

Organization

"Honestly, a Christmas meal like that is a real gift."
Catherine, who likes to flatter

The evening before, you can...
· Make the candied orange peel.

A few hours before, you can...
· Make the potato mille-feuilles and the sauce.
· Soak the morels in water.
· Make the chocolate tart.

Just before your guests arrive, you can...
· Cook the duck breasts, reducing the cooking time by 3 minutes and then reheating them in the oven at 320 °F (160 °C) for 7 minutes.

Potato and smoked salmon mille-feuilles

Ingredients
· 8 large potatoes
· I tbsp salt
· I lemon
· 2 cups (500 ml) thick crème fraîche or sour cream
· 8 sprigs dill
· 16 slices smoked salmon
· 3 oz (80g) salmon roe

Equipment
· I potato peeler
· I large saucepan
· I lemon squeezer

How long it will take
30 minutes preparation time
+ 30 minutes cooking time

Method
Peel the potatoes. In a large saucepan, bring some water to a boil with a tablespoon of salt. Add the potatoes. After 20 minutes, start checking to see if they are done by prodding them with the point of a knife. When the point goes in easily, they are done. Lift out of the water and allow to cool slightly. While the potatoes are cooking, halve the lemon, squeeze the juice into a bowl, and combine with the crème fraîche or sour cream. Wash and dry the dill. When the potatoes are cool enough to handle, cut them carefully into wide slices. Cut the slices of smoked salmon into pieces to fit the potatoes. Layer up the smoked salmon slices between the potato slices, then place the mille-feuilles on plates, spoon the cream around, and garnish with the salmon roe and dill.

Duck breasts with foie gras and morels

Ingredients

- 3 cups (100 g) dried morels
- 8 shallots
- 1/2 lemon
- 4 duck breasts
- 2 cups (500 ml) light cream
- 4 slices foie gras (about 14 oz/400 g)
- 3 tsp butter
- Salt and pepper

Equipment

- 1 lemon squeezer
- 1 or 2 nonstick skillets
- aluminum foil
- 1 large saucepan

How long it will take

2 hours soaking time for the morels
+ 20 minutes preparation time
+30 minutes cooking time

Method

Put the morels to soak in water at least 2 hours before you are going to cook them. Peel and halve the shallots. With flat side down, slice finely, then cut each slice at right angles to produce small dice. Squeeze the half lemon. Get out the duck breasts and place them with the skin (the fatty side) facing up. Using a knife, score the skin to create a lattice pattern. The cuts should be about 1/8 inch (3 mm) deep to let the fat run out freely while cooking. If your kitchen has a window, open it, and shut the door, because the duck will smoke while cooking. Heat the skillet(s) over a high heat. When really hot, add the duck breasts, skin (fatty) side down. Season the flesh side of the duck with salt and pepper. If you are using just one skillet, you will have to cook the duck breasts in two batches, covering the first batch with aluminum foil to keep it hot.

It will take about 10 minutes to cook the skin side. The duck breasts will produce a lot of fat. Pour it off as and when you need to. After 10 minutes, turn the duck breasts over and cook for an additional 5 minutes. While the duck breasts are cooking, drain the morels. In a saucepan, melt the butter over a low heat, add the chopped shallots and let cook for 2 minutes, then add the morels and the lemon juice. Add salt and cook for 10 minutes. Remove the pan from the heat.

When the duck breasts are cooked, transfer them to a plate and allow to rest for 5 minutes, covering them with aluminum foil, so that the meat relaxes and becomes more tender. Pour the cream into one of the skillets, then add the slices of foie gras. Season with salt and pepper and cook over a

moderate heat until the foie gras has melted and the sauce is smooth. Slice the duck breasts. Pour the sauce onto plates, arrange a sliced half duck breast on each plate, add the morels, and serve.

Chocolate and candied orange tart

Ingredients

- 3/4 cup (200 ml) water
- 1/2 cup (100 g) superfine sugar
- 3 non-waxed oranges
- 1 round ready-rolled sweet short pastry
- 1 jar orange marmalade
- 1 2/3 cups (400 ml) light cream
- 10 oz (300 g) bittersweet chocolate (at least 60% cocoa solids)
- 5 tbsp (70 g) butter

Equipment

- 1 large tart pan
- 1 whisk

How long it will take

30 minutes preparation time
+ 1 hour cooking time

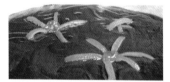

Method

Preheat the oven to 350 °F (180 °C). Put the water and sugar in a saucepan and bring to simmering point. Finely slice the oranges, remove the flesh, and cut the peel into strips, taking care to get rid of as much of the white pith as possible. Put the orange strips into the sugar syrup and allow to cook for between 15 and 30 minutes until the white part beneath the peel becomes slightly transparent. Meanwhile, line the tart pan with the pastry, leaving it on the packing paper. Prick the base with a fork, then bake for 20 minutes until the pastry is cooked. Remove from the oven and allow to cool. Spread the marmalade over the base of the pastry case, reserving 1 tablespoon for decoration. Break the chocolate into small pieces and melt with the butter in a saucepan over a very low heat or in a microwave oven for 30 seconds at a time. Carefully pour the cream over the melted chocolate and butter mixture, beating to produce a very smooth cream. Transfer this mixture to the pastry case. Place in the refrigera-

tor for about 2 hours. Just before serving, drain the orange strips and arrange them attractively over the tart together with a little of the reserved marmalade.

Surprise parcels dinner

or

how to transform your meal into a game show

Soft goat cheese stuffed tomatoes

Salmon, leek, and orange parcels

Crêpe moneybags with Nutella mousse

Each dish looks like a parcel, the contents of which you have to discover. But have no qualms, your guests won't be in for any unpleasant surprises. What is hiding beneath the tomato lid? What are they going to find in the parcel that glistens? And what will be revealed when they undo the string of the crêpes moneybag? You can make your guests play, it's a sort of cookery guessing game. Will the winner earn the right to seconds, or the right to come back next week? You are the game show host!

Organization

"Fish in a parcel, it's sumptuous, superbly good, and I get the impression that it's not complicated."
Bernard, an expert cookery analyst

The evening before, you can…

· Make the Nutella mousse.
· Make the crêpe batter.

A few hours before, you can…

· Make the stuffed tomatoes.
· Make the crêpes for the moneybags.

· Make the salmon parcels, then keep them in the refrigerator.

"And what's more, you can play games at the table!"
Pierre, a fan of Who Wants to be a Millionaire

Just before your guests arrive, you can…

· Make up the crêpe money-bags.

"I didn't guess anything, but I ate everything up."
Étienne, who didn't tax her brains

Soft goat cheese stuffed tomatoes

Ingredients

· 8 tomatoes
· 16 shelled walnut halves
· 2 shallots
· 8 dried figs
· 14 oz (400 g) Chavroux or other soft goat cheese
· 8 sprigs tarragon (or cilantro, chervil, etc.)

Equipment

None

How long it will take

30 minutes preparation time

Method

Cut the tomatoes so as to make a lid. Using a teaspoon, carefully remove the flesh and seeds of the tomatoes and discard, then place the tomatoes upside down to allow the juice to run out. Break the walnuts into small pieces. Peel the shallots, trimming the tops and bottoms and removing the dried skin. Cut them in half, place them on their flat side, and slice finely, then cut each slice again at right angles so as to produce small dice. Cut the figs into small pieces too. Combine the goat cheese with the walnuts, shallots, and figs and spoon this mixture into the tomatoes. Lay a sprig of herbs on top and replace the tomato lids. That's it!

Salmon, leek, and orange parcels

Ingredients
- 8 leeks
- 4 oranges
- 16 tbsp olive oil
- 8 salmon steaks, skin removed
- 4 tbsp balsamic vinegar
- Salt and pepper

Equipment
- 1 large saucepan
- 1 zester or 1 potato peeler
- 1 lemon squeezer
- aluminum foil
- 1 baking sheet

Preparation time
30 minutes preparation + 15 minutes cooking

Method
Preheat the oven to 465 °F (240 °C). Trim the base of the white part of the leeks, then cut off the green part where it begins to separate into large strips. Remove the first layer of skin. Wash the leeks well under running water, then dry. Bring some water to a boil in a large saucepan. When it boils, add the leeks and cook for 5 minutes. If they are too long to fit, cut them in half. Drain the leeks and allow to cool. Wash and dry the oranges. Using a zester or potato peeler, remove broad strips of peel, then cut them into fine strips. Squeeze the oranges. Combine the juice with the olive oil, then set aside half of this sauce. When the leeks are just warm, slice them up very finely. Tear off eight pieces of aluminum foil, each measuring 16 inches (40 cm). Lay them flat, shiny side down. Arrange the sliced leeks in the center of the foil and top with the salmon steaks. Season with salt and pepper. Pour the remaining orange sauce over the salmon and leeks. Sprinkle with the strips of orange zest. Seal the aluminum foil

74

by folding over the edges several times so that the parcels are completely airtight (this is very important to keep the flavors in). Place the parcels on a baking sheet and bake in the oven for 10 minutes. If they won't all fit on the baking sheet, cook them in two batches. While they are cooking, add the balsamic vinegar to the reserved orange and olive oil sauce and combine. Remove the parcels from the oven. Place them on plates and serve immediately, with the sauce alongside.

Crêpe moneybags
with Nutella mousse

Ingredients

• 10 eggs
• 1 cup (200 g) Nutella or other hazelnut and chocolate spread
• 2 tsp butter
• 1 1/3 cups (150 g) flour
• 1 1/4 cups (300 ml) milk
• 2 tbsp oil (to fry the pancakes)
• Salt

Equipment

• 1 small saucepan
• 2 large mixing bowls
• 1 electric beater
• 1 large nonstick skillet
• 1 large spatula
• 8 ribbons to tie around the moneybags

How long it will take

40 minutes preparation time the evening before or in the morning
+ 12 hours chilling time
+ 20 minutes cooking time on the day itself

Method

Break eight eggs and separate the whites from the yolks, reserving all the whites and only four yolks. Melt the Nutella in a small saucepan over a very low heat. When it has become really runny, remove it from the heat, pour into a mixing bowl, and combine with the four egg yolks. Add a pinch of salt to the egg whites and beat until they turn white. Continue beating until they are very firm and form stiff peaks that hold their shape. Carefully fold the egg whites into the Nutella, a little at a time. When they are thoroughly combined, place in the refrigerator for at least 12 hours. To make the crêpe batter, melt 2 teaspoons of butter over a low heat. Pour the flour, milk, the two remaining eggs, the melted butter, and a pinch of salt into a mixing bowl and beat until smooth. Allow the mixture to rest for at least 1 hour. Heat a skillet over a moderate heat with a little oil. Add a small glassful of the

crêpe mixture. Tilt the skillet to spread out the batter. Wait until the crêpe is cooked on one side: the edges should be golden and should lift up slightly. Turn the crêpe over using a spatula and cook the other side. Cook eight crêpes, adding more oil to the skillet if necessary. Allow them to cool, then fill with the Nutella mousse, draw up the sides, and tie with a ribbon.

Soup soup soup supper

or

how to be sure of growing well

 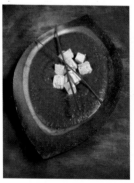 

Tomato and red pep-per soup with cheese and herb chips

Cream of lentil soup with diced foie gras

Chocolate and ginger soup with litchis

"Eat up your soup, it will make you grow!" You will have heard that yourself once upon a time. And that proves it—you have grown up. So soup can no longer work its magic. But that's no reason to deprive yourself of the pleasure of a good soup, hot and comforting in winter, cold and refreshing in summer. Soup comes in many forms, from very light and clear to creamy and thick, smooth or with bits in, and in all sorts of colors. And as for the ingredients, you are spoilt for choice: from the humble potato to the most luxurious lobster. A menu consisting solely of soup may seem rather over the top, but it is not monotonous in the slightest, neither on the eyes, nor on the taste buds. So get out your spoons and enjoy!

"Slurp, slurp, slurp."
Maurice, not very well brought up

"I was worried, because I don't really like soup, but everything was delicious."
Sarah, extremely relieved

Organization

The evening before, you can...

· Make the tomato soup.
· Make the lentil soup.
· Make the chocolate soup.

"To be honest, I wouldn't have dared serve up nothing but soup, but it made a real dinner."
Manu, not exactly reckless

A few hours before, you can...

· Make the cheese chips
· Peel the litchis and remove the pits.

Just before your guests arrive, you can...

· Dice the foie gras.

Tomato and red pepper soup with cheese and herb chips

Ingredients

· 16 tomatoes
· 8 red bell peppers
· 16 shallots
· 4 tbsp oil
· 1 tbsp superfine sugar
· 2 cups (500 ml) water
· 1/4 lb (100 g) Mimolette or cheddar cheese
· 1 tbsp flour
· 8 leaves basil or 8 blades of chive
· Salt and pepper

Equipment

· 1 large saucepan or 1 heatproof casserole dish with lid
· 1 cheese grater
· 1 nonstick skillet
· paper towels
· 1 blender

How long it will take

30 minutes preparation time
+ 40 minutes cooking time

Method

Wash the tomatoes and cut them into quarters. Remove the seeds and juice. Wash the bell peppers and cut off the stalk with a knife. Cut the peppers into four. Remove the seeds and the white membranes using a knife. Cut the flesh into large pieces. Peel the shallots, cut them in half, place them flat side down, and slice. Pour the oil into the saucepan and heat over a low heat. Add the sliced shallots and cook for 5 minutes until they are transparent. Add the chopped tomatoes, peppers, sugar, and water. Season well with salt and pepper. Cover and allow to cook for 30 minutes. The liquid should simmer gently. When the vegetables are cooked, grate the cheese and combine with the flour. Wash and finely slice the herbs. Heat the skillet over a high heat. Place a paper towel on a plate. Place 4 tablespoons of grated cheese in the skillet in four separate piles and spread them out to form four circles. Sprinkle a few herbs over each circle.

When the cheese melts, becomes translucent, bubbles, and is beautifully golden around the edges, remove the chips very carefully with a spatula (and a tablespoon if necessary) and place them on the paper towel. Repeat the process until you have eight chips. (Be warned, the cheese can produce a strong smell when cooking, so it is advisable to open a window.) When the vegetables are cooked, process them in a blender to produce a smooth mixture. Taste, adding salt and pepper if necessary. Serve the soup hot or cold, according to taste, with the cheese and herb chips.

Cream of lentil soup with diced foie gras

Ingredients

· 6 shallots
· 1 carrot
· 1 tbsp butter
· 5 cups (1 kg) green French lentils
· 12 1/2 cups (3.1 liters) water
· 4 tbsp balsamic vinegar
· 8 slices foie gras
· 16 sprigs chives
· Salt and pepper

Equipment

· 1 potato peeler
· 1 large saucepan or 1 heatproof casserole dish with lid
· 1 blender

How long it will take

20 minutes preparation time
+ 1 hour cooking time

Method

Peel and finely slice the shallots. Peel and slice the carrot. Melt the butter in a saucepan or casserole dish over a low heat. Add the shallots and cook for 5 minutes, without letting them brown. Add the lentils, carrot, and water. Bring to a boil, then reduce the heat, and cook, covered, over a low heat for 45 minutes. Season with salt and pepper. When cooked, process in a blender together with the balsamic vinegar. When ready to serve, rinse out the saucepan or casserole dish, return the cream of lentil soup to the pan and heat over a low heat. Taste, adding more salt or pepper if necessary. Add more water if the soup is too thick. Dice the foie gras. Wash and dry the chives. Pour the cream of lentil soup into bowls, sprinkle with the diced foie gras, and garnish with the chives.

Chocolate and ginger soup with litchis

Ingredients
· 24 fresh or canned litchis
· I small piece fresh gingerroot or I tbsp ground ginger
· 3/4 lb (350 g) bittersweet chocolate
· I 1/4 cups (300 ml) light cream
· 3 cups (700 ml) milk

Equipment
· I potato peeler
· 2 saucepans
· I hand beater

How long it will take
15 minutes preparation time
+ 10 minutes cooking time

Method
If using fresh litchis, peel them and remove the pits; if using canned litchis, drain them. If using fresh gingerroot, peel it using a potato peeler, then cut into roughly 1/8 inch (3 mm) thick slices. Break the chocolate into small pieces, then melt in a saucepan over a very low heat, or in a microwave oven, 30 seconds at a time (stirring gently after each blast). Transfer to a mixing bowl and allow to cool slightly. In a saucepan, heat the cream, milk, and ground or sliced ginger over a high heat. When it boils, remove the sliced ginger and pour the contents of the pan over the melted chocolate, beating constantly. Allow to cool slightly. If you have made the soup in advance and it has cooled, reheat it gently to serve it warm. Pour the soup into shallow bowls and arrange the litchis on top at the last minute.

Bistro supper

or

bring out the checkered tablecloths

Terrine of leeks with French dressing

Meat and potato pie

Vanilla rice pudding

From time to time, you want to give your brain and your taste buds a rest. Having been tempted by dishes with ever more complicated names, with unknown flavors, in all sorts of strange shapes and forms, you now desire only one thing: traditional cooking with no surprises. People no longer dare to serve these bistro dishes; nowadays it is the thing to know how to demonstrate a creative and modern style in the kitchen. However, a good roast chicken (we don't eat it very often), a homemade egg mayonnaise, leeks with French dressing, or a baked custard, frankly, they're delicious. A dish doesn't have to be sophisticated to be good. The great cooks stand out not only for their inventiveness, but also for their ability to raise ordinary dishes to new dizzing heights. Joël Robuchon, one of France's most famous chefs, has nonetheless restored acclaim to the humble mashed potato, much to the greater happiness of the clients at his three-star restaurant. The menu suggested here has no ambition other than to see your guests lick their lips and pat their stomachs.

Organization

The evening before, you can…
· Make the leek terrine and the dressing.
· Prepare the pie without cooking it.
Keep both dishes in the refrigerator.

"Why go out to a bistro when you can eat like that with friends?" Christophe, who has a highly developed practical bent

A few hours before, you can…
· Make the rice pudding
Just before your guests arrive, you can…
· Slice the leek terrine.

"Nearly as good as the meat and potato pie my granny used to make." Gaspard, rather nostalgic

87

Terrine of leeks with French dressing

Ingredients

· 12 leeks (you can buy just the white parts, ready trimmed, with the green parts removed)
· 1 oz (24 g) unsweetened gelatin (for example, Madeira-flavored gelatin)
· 1 2/3 cups (400 ml) water
· 16 blades of chive
· 3 tsp mustard
· 3 tbsp vinegar
· 9 tbsp oil
· Salt and pepper

Equipment

· 1 loaf pan
· 1 large saucepan
· plastic wrap

How long it will take

20 minutes preparation time
+ 20 minutes cooking time the evening before or the morning
+ 12 hours setting time

Method

Cut the leeks to the same length as the loaf pan. If your saucepan is not big enough, cut the leeks in half again. Trim the end of the white part of the leeks, then cut the green part where it begins to separate out into large leaves. Remove the first layer of skin and wash well under running water. Bring a large saucepan of salted water to a boil. When it reaches a rolling boil, producing large bubbles, add the leeks and cook for 20 minutes. Drain thoroughly, pressing down on the leeks to extract the water, then allow to cool. Make up the gelatin, using 1 2/3 cups (400 ml) water, following the manufacturer's instructions on the package. Wash and dry the chives, then cut into small pieces. Line the loaf pan with plastic wrap. Pour in the first, thin layer of jelly. Sprinkle with a third of the chives. Arrange four leeks on top. Add more jelly, sprinkle with another third of the chives, and arrange the remaining leeks on top. Add more jelly and the rest of the chives, and place in the refrigerator for at least 12 hours to set.

In a bowl, combine the mustard, vinegar, and salt. Add 3 tablespoons of oil and mix again. The dressing should be quite smooth. Mix in the remaining oil. Finally, stir in some pepper. When ready to serve, turn the terrine out onto a dish. Cut into slices using a large knife. Hold the terrine with a piece of plastic wrap to prevent it from disintegrating—not that it matters if it does. Arrange the slices on plates and spoon over a little French dressing.

Meat and potato pie

Ingredients
- 3 1/4 lb (1.5 kg) potatoes (for the mashed potato)
- 1 1/4 cups (300 ml) milk
- 6 tbsp (100 ml) light cream
- 1/2 cup (125 g) butter
- 3 onions
- 2 1/4 lb (1 kg) ground beef
- 1/2 cup (140 g) tomato paste
- 1 cup (120 g) grated Emmental cheese
- Salt and pepper

Equipment
- 1 potato peeler
- 2 large saucepans or 2 heatproof casserole dishes
- 1 sieve
- 1 potato masher (use a fork if you do not have a masher)
- 1 large ovenproof dish

How long it will take
40 minutes preparation time
+ 1 hour cooking time

Method
Peel the potatoes and cut them into pieces roughly 3/4 inch (2 cm) square. Put them in a large saucepan or casserole dish full of cold water with a tablespoon of salt. Bring the water to a boil and allow to cook for 20 minutes. Check to see if the potatoes are cooked by pricking them with the point of a knife. It should go in easily. Drain the potatoes and return them to the pan or casserole dish. Add the milk, the cream, and half the butter. Reheat gently and mash, using the potato masher or a fork, until the mixture is smooth. Season with salt and pepper. Peel the onions, removing the dry skin layer. Cut them in half, place them flat side down, and slice finely. Heat 1 tablespoon of butter in a large saucepan or casserole dish over a moderate heat. When the butter has melted, add the sliced onion. Sprinkle with salt and cook for 5 minutes. Add the ground beef and the tomato paste, and cook for about 20 minutes more, stirring well so that all the meat cooks.

Preheat the oven to 350 °F (180 °C). Grease the ovenproof dish by spreading a little butter using a piece of paper towel. Spread out half the mashed potato over the base to form the first layer, then add the meat, and top with the remaining mashed potato. Cut the remaining butter into small pieces, dot them over the top, then sprinkle with the grated cheese. Bake for 15 minutes. Serve very hot.

Vanilla rice pudding

Ingredients
· 8 cups (2 liters) milk
· 2 vanilla beans
· 3 cups (500 g) short-grain rice (Italian risotto rice is best, as it is very moist)
· 1/2 cup (100 g) butter
· Scant 1 cup (200 g) superfine sugar
· Salt

Equipment
· 1 large saucepan

How long it will take
5 minutes preparation time
+ 40 minutes cooking time

Method
Bring the milk to a boil. Split the vanilla beans lengthwise using a pointed knife. Scrape out the insides and put the black seeds and the empty beans into the milk. Add the rice, butter, and a pinch of salt to the boiling milk. Reduce the heat and cook over a low heat for 15 minutes, stirring frequently. Then add the sugar and continue to cook for an additional 20 minutes, still stirring frequently. When cooked, remove the vanilla beans. Serve the rice pudding cold or warm.

Totally raw dinner

or

nothing is cooked, everything's cold

Cucumber boats with smoked salmon mousse

Duck and turnip carpaccio

Strawberry and melon tartare with port

If ever your oven breaks down and, woe upon woe, your burners no longer work, with this menu and against all the odds, you can still have guests round to dinner. Even if the circumstances are less "dramatic," there are times when you just want a totally no-cook meal. In the summer, for example, when it is very hot, it is pleasant for your guests to eat cold and it is also pleasant for you to cook cold, with no skillet, no saucepan, etc., just equipped with your knife. What's more, it's a trend, the totally raw: there are restaurants now whose sole theme is "raw." They boast the beneficial effects on the body of food that has not been altered by cooking.

Organization

The evening before, you can…
· Make the smoked salmon mousse.

A few hours before, you can…
· Make the cucumber boats.
· Make the duck and turnip carpaccio.
· Make the strawberry and melon tartare.

Just before your guests arrive, you can…
· Fill the cucumber boats.
· Arrange the carpaccios on plates.

Cucumber boats with smoked salmon mousse

Ingredients

· 2 preserved lemons (or 2 lemons)
· 10 slices smoked salmon
· 1 1/4 cups (300 g) fromage frais or cream cheese
· 2 cucumbers
· 4 sprigs cilantro (or chives)

Equipment

· 1 lemon squeezer (optional)
· 1 blender
· 1 potato peeler

How long it will take

30 minutes preparation time

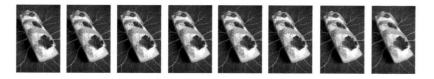

Method

If using preserved lemons, cut them into very small cubes. If using ordinary lemons, squeeze them. Cut eight slices of smoked salmon into broad strips and place in the blender with the fromage frais or cream cheese. Blend until the mixture is smooth. Combine with the diced preserved lemons or the lemon juice. Cut the remaining smoked salmon into thin strips. Cut off the ends of the cucumbers. Cut the cucumbers in two lengthwise, then across. Peel these eight pieces of cucumber, then hollow them out, using a spoon to remove the seeds, and make the boats. Fill the boats with the salmon mousse and garnish with the strips of smoked salmon. When ready to serve, wash and dry the herbs, and arrange over the boats.

Duck and turnip carpaccio

Ingredients

· I lemon
· 6 tbsp hazelnut oil (or olive oil)
· 6 tbsp honey
· 4 duck breast fillets
· 6 baby turnips
· I tbsp cumin seeds
· Salt and pepper

Equipment

· I lemon squeezer
· I large, sharp knife
· plastic wrap

How long it will take

30 minutes preparation time
+ at least 2 hours chilling time

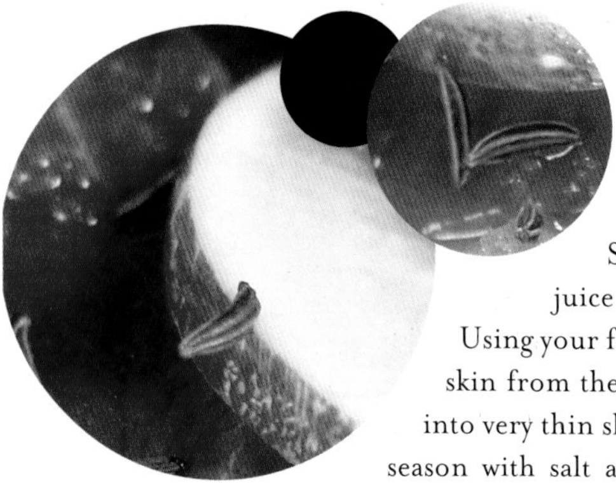

Method

Squeeze the lemon. Combine the juice with the hazelnut oil and honey. Using your fingers or a knife, remove the fatty skin from the duck breasts. Cut the duck flesh into very thin slices. Arrange them on a dish and season with salt and pepper. Pour half the sauce over the meat, cover with plastic wrap, and put in the refrigerator. Wash and finely slice the turnips. Put them in a mixing bowl, sprinkle with salt, and combine with the remaining sauce. Place in the refrigerator for at least 2 hours. When chilled, arrange the duck and turnip slices on plates, sprinkle with a few cumin seeds, and serve immediately.

Strawberry and melon tartare with port

Ingredients

- 1 lemon
- 8 tbsp honey
- 8 tbsp port
- 3 1/3 cups (500 g) strawberries
- 2 melons
- Mint leaves, to decorate (optional)

Equipment

- 1 lemon squeezer

How long it will take

20 minutes preparation time

Method

Cut the lemon in half and squeeze to produce 4 tablespoons of juice. Combine the juice with the honey and port. Quickly wash the strawberries under running water, dry them, and cut into small dice. Cut the melons into four and remove the seeds using a tablespoon. Using a knife, remove the melon skin. Cut the flesh into small dice the same size as the diced strawberries. Combine the fruits with the sauce in a large serving bowl. Decorate, if desired, with the mint leaves.

Vegetarian dinner

or

no meat, no poultry, and not even any fish

Cream of endive and blue cheese soup

Crispy eggplant with feta cheese

Coconut tartlets with sautéed mango

Even if you yourself are not devoted body and soul to the protection of animals, it can happen that there are vegetarians among your guests. Most restaurants now provide vegetarian dishes on the menu. Before throwing yourself into the kitchen, it's best to check how strict your vegetarian friend is. Will it be enough just to rule out meat, poultry, and fish, or will you also have to exclude eggs and dairy produce? There are some people who only refuse to eat four-legged creatures, so they can eat poultry and fish. The menu presented here is in line with the most common vegetarian diets: it includes dairy produce and eggs.

Organization

"Fruit and vegetables are good for your health, so I'm all for it."
Édouard, who is often all for it anyway

The evening before, you can...
· Make the cream of endive soup, omitting the cream.
· Make the bases for the coconut tartlets; store them in a cool, dry place.

A few hours before, you can...
· Dice the blue cheese
· Prepare the eggplants, but do not bake for the second time yet.
· Prepare the mangoes, but do not sauté them yet.

"Eight people for dinner, that makes for really lively conversation."
Jules, pleased to make new friends

Cream of endive and blue cheese soup

Ingredients
- 2 onions
- 16 Belgian endives
- 4 tsp butter
- 2 oranges
- 5 oz (150 g) blue cheese, such as bleu d'Auvergne
- 2 cups (500 ml) light cream
- 1 tbsp superfine sugar
- Salt and pepper

Equipment
- 1 large saucepan or 1 heatproof casserole dish
- 1 zester or 1 potato peeler
- 1 lemon squeezer
- 1 blender

How long it will take
30 minutes preparation time
+ 30 minutes cooking time

Method
Peel the onions, cutting and removing the dry skin. Cut them in half, place them flat side down, and slice. Cut the base of the endives about 1 inch (3 cm) up and remove the external leaves if they are damaged. (There's no need to wash the endives.) Cut the endives into 3/4 inch (2 cm) thick slices. Heat the butter in a large saucepan over a low heat. When it has melted, add the endive chunks and onion slices, and sprinkle with salt. Cook for 25 minutes, stirring from time to time, until the endives are really transparent and soft. They will release water and reduce during cooking. Don't worry, it's normal. Meanwhile, thoroughly wash and then dry the oranges. Using a zester, remove thin strips of zest. If using a potato peeler, peel off eight long pieces of peel and cut them into very thin strips about 1/16 inch (1 mm) wide. Cut the oranges in two and squeeze them. Cut the cheese into small cubes. After 25 minutes, add the orange juice to the pan and cook for an additional 5 minutes.

When cooked, process in a blender. Rinse out the saucepan. Return the blended endives to the pan, add the cream, and heat over a low heat. Check the seasoning, adding the sugar if it is a little bitter and a little salt if necessary. Add some pepper. Pour into bowls and sprinkle with the cubes of cheese and the strips of orange zest. Serve immediately.

Crispy eggplant with feta cheese

Ingredients
· 4 eggplants
· 2 garlic cloves
· 1 3/4 lb (800 g) feta cheese
· 16 tbsp rolled oats
· 16 tbsp olive oil
· 6 cups (300 g) arugula (or any other leaf salad)
· 8 tbsp balsamic vinegar

Equipment
· 1 large ovenproof dish

How long it will take
30 minutes preparation time
+ 55 minutes cooking time

Method
Preheat the oven to 400 °F (200 °C). Wash the eggplants and cut them in half lengthwise. Arrange them in a large dish and bake for 30 minutes. Trim the ends of the garlic cloves and remove the papery skin. Cut the flesh into small dice. After 30 minutes, remove the eggplants from the oven and allow them to cool slightly. Using a tablespoon, scoop out the flesh from the eggplants, taking care not to break the skin. Chop the eggplant flesh into small dice and combine with the feta and garlic. Fill the eggplant cases with this mixture. Sprinkle 2 tablespoons of rolled oats over each half eggplant and drizzle each with a tablespoon of olive oil. Return to the oven to bake for an additional 20 minutes. Meanwhile, wash and dry the arugula if necessary. Combine the remaining 8 tablespoons of olive oil with 8 tablespoons of balsamic vinegar. Toss the salad with the dressing. After the 20 minutes, place the eggplants under a hot broiler until they are beautifully golden (about 3–5 minutes). Serve the eggplants with the salad.

Coconut tartlets with sautéed mango

Ingredients

• 2 eggs
• 1 cup + 1 tbsp (240 g) superfine sugar for the tartlets
• 3 cups (250 g) shredded coconut
• 6 mangoes
• 1 tbsp butter
• 6 tbsp superfine sugar for cooking the mangoes

Equipment

• 1 baking sheet, preferably non-stick. If not, line with some parchment paper
• 1 hand beater
• 1 large nonstick skillet

How long it will take

40 minutes preparation time
+ 25 minutes cooking time

Method

If your baking sheet is not nonstick, cover it with parchment paper. Preheat the oven to 265 °F (130 °C). Break the eggs into a mixing bowl and beat. Add the quantity of sugar for the tartlets and beat well again. Then add the shredded coconut (reserving 4 tablespoons to decorate the tartlets), and beat again. Spoon half the coconut mixture into four small mounds on the baking sheet, then press them down to form four circles. Put in the oven and bake for 10–15 minutes, keeping a watchful eye on the tartlets. As soon as the circles are lightly golden, remove them from the oven. Allow to cool completely before carefully removing from the baking sheet. Repeat with the second batch of the mixture. Slice the mango flesh as close as possible to the pit, peel the pieces you slice off, and cut them into small dice. Heat the skillet over a high heat. When it is hot, melt the butter and add the 6 tablespoons of superfine sugar.

When the sugar is very hot, add the mango pieces to the skillet, and cook, stir-ring them from time to time, for about 10 minutes, until they are nicely gold-en. Reduce the heat if it gets too hot. Place the coconut tartlets on plates, spoon the diced mango on top, and sprinkle with a little shredded coconut.

All cheese dinner

or

thank you to the Moo Moos, Baa Baas, and Maa Maas!

Tomato crumble with mature cheese and pine nuts

Roast beef and gnocchi with Gorgonzola cream sauce

Cream cheese tart

Animals give us generous quantities of milk, and for centuries man has transformed it into cheese. You can eat it in the traditional way, on a cheese board either before or after dessert. There is such a wide variety to choose from, with over four hundred in France alone! Fresh, very ripe, mild, smelly, some even very smelly, small, large, round, oval, soft, hard, dry, holey, runny—the list is endless. And more and more people are using cheese for cooking. Hot cheese is heavenly, it pulls into threads, it melts, it turns runny, and it smells delicious from appetizer to dessert.

"Dinner parties with my friends, that's what I like best in all the world." Nicolas, a good friend

Organization

The evening before, you can…
· Make the crumble mixture, storing it overnight in the refrigerator.

A few hours before the meal, you can…
· Make the crumble ready to pop it in the oven later.
· Make the cream cheese tart.

"I love cheese, it's just sooo good." Dorothée, a confirmed caseophile

"My favorite cheese is a dry goat cheese. I also like properly ripe Camembert. Oh, and Comté fully matured for at least 12 months… In a nutshell, an all cheese dinner is the perfect choice." Alain, who is almost in seventh heaven

Tomato crumble with mature cheese and pine nuts

Ingredients

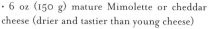

· 6 oz (150 g) mature Mimolette or cheddar cheese (drier and tastier than young cheese)
· 12 tomatoes
· 4 tbsp olive oil
· 8 tbsp balsamic vinegar
· 2/3 cup (150 g) butter
· 1 1/4 cups (150 g) flour
· 2 handfuls pine nuts (alternatively, you can use walnuts broken into small pieces)

Equipment

· 1 cheese grater
· 1 large ovenproof dish or 8 ramekin dishes
· 1 large mixing bowl

How long it will take

30 minutes preparation time
+ 30 minutes cooking time

Method

Preheat the oven to 350 °F (180 °C). Grate the cheese. Wash and dry the tomatoes, then cut each tomato into eight pieces and remove the seeds. Cut each slice of tomato into four to produce small dice. Spread the oil over the base of the ovenproof dish. Put the diced tomatoes in the dish, sprinkle with salt, pour over the balsamic vinegar, and stir. Cut the butter in small pieces. Put the butter, flour, and cheese into a large mixing bowl. Using the fingertips, blend the butter into the flour until all the ingredients are thoroughly incorporated. The result should resemble bread crumbs—don't try to produce a smooth mixture. Spoon this mixture over the tomatoes to form a crust and sprinkle with the pine nuts. When the oven has reached the correct temperature, put the dish in the oven and cook for about 30 minutes or until the crust is beautifully golden. Take a look in the oven from time to time to check that the crumble is not burn-

ing. If it is, reduce the oven temperature to 300 °F (150 °C) and continue cooking. On the other hand, if after 20 minutes it is still not golden, increase the temperature to 400 °F (200 °C). When it is ready, remove the dish from the oven, allow to cool for 5 minutes, then serve.

Roast beef and gnocchi with Gorgonzola cream sauce

Ingredients

· 1 beef roasting joint weighing about 3 lb 5 oz (1.5 kg)
· 2 tbsp oil
· 3 lb 5 oz (1.5 kg) gnocchi (fresh Italian pasta made from potatoes—you'll find it in specialty Italian stores or on the fresh pasta aisle in the supermarket)
· 1/2 lb (250 g) Gorgonzola cheese (a very creamy blue Italian cheese)
· 3 cups (750 ml) light cream
· Salt

Equipment

· 1 large ovenproof dish
· aluminum foil
· 1 large saucepan or 1 casserole dish
· 1 small saucepan
· 1 sieve
· 1 large sharp knife

How long it will take

10 minutes preparation time
+ 1 hour cooking time

Method

If possible, take the meat out of the refrigerator an hour before cooking. Preheat the oven to 465 °F (240 °C). Brush the oil over the baking dish. Place the meat in the dish, sprinkle with salt, and put it in the oven for 10 minutes to brown, then reduce the heat to 400 °F (200 °C) and cook for an additional 40 minutes. When the meat is cooked, cover with aluminum foil and let rest for 10–15 minutes before carving. While the meat is resting, bring a large saucepan of water to a boil with 2 tablespoons of salt, then add the gnocchi. They are ready when they return to the surface—this takes about 3 minutes. When they are cooked, drain them. Put the cheese and the cream in a saucepan, melt over a moderate heat, and stir. Add the meat juices to this sauce. Carve the roasting joint into slices, return them to the dish, and serve with the gnocchi and sauce.

Cream cheese tart

Ingredients

- 1 lemon
- 3/4 cup (200 g) Kiri, Saint Moret, or other cream cheese
- 5 eggs
- 1 cup (250 g) fromage blanc or Quark
- Scant 1 cup (200 g) superfine sugar
- 3 tbsp (50 ml) cognac (optional)
- 1 round ready-rolled short crust pastry
- 1 handful raisins

Equipment

- 1 lemon squeezer
- 1 electric or hand beater
- 1 large tart pan

How long it will take

20 minutes preparation time
+ 45 minutes cooking time

Method

Preheat the oven to 430 °F (220 °C). Squeeze the lemon. Beat together all the ingredients, apart from the pastry and the raisins, until the mixture is very smooth. Spread the pastry round over the base of the tart pan, leaving it on the packing paper. Fill the lined tart pan with the cheese mixture, sprinkle with the raisins, and bake in the oven for 40 minutes. The top should turn pale golden (if it turns brown, reduce the oven temperature to 350 °F (180 °C). Remove from the oven. Allow to cool before turning out carefully.

All green dinner

or

the hope that everything will turn out well

Lima beans with yogurt, herbs, and lime

Chicken scallops with pesto and green beans

Green apple and kiwi fruit salad

Green is the color of hope. It also symbolizes the natural world that surrounds us and which is full to overflowing with good things for us to eat. It is the symbolic color of ecology. Green is grass in the garden, leaves on the trees, ferns... And it is also peas, aromatic herbs, green beans, broccoli, Romanesca cauliflower...

Organization

A few hours before the meal, you can ...

· Make the yogurt sauce and cook the lima beans.

· Cook the green beans; you can reheat them with the butter later.

· Make the fruit salad, but leave out the mint until later.

Just before your guests arrive, you can ...

· Cook the chicken scallops: just pop them in the oven.

Lima beans with yogurt, herbs, and lime

Ingredients

- 3 1/2 cups (600 g) frozen lima beans
- 16 sprigs cilantro
- 16 basil leaves
- 16 blades of chive (don't worry if you can't find all the herbs, you can use others instead or just use more of the ones you have)
- 2 limes
- 4 small cartons plain whole milk yogurt
- 4 tbsp olive oil
- Salt

Equipment

- 1 large saucepan
- 1 sieve
- 1 zester or 1 potato peeler
- 1 lemon squeezer
- 1 blender

How long it will take

20 minutes preparation time
+ 5 minutes cooking time

Method

Bring a large saucepan of water to a boil, add the lima beans while still frozen, and cook for 5 minutes. Drain and allow to cool. Wash, dry, and remove the leaves of the herbs, setting some aside for the garnish. Using the zester, remove the zest from the limes, or peel off strips of zest using a potato peeler and then cut them into fine shreds. Squeeze the limes. Blend the yogurt with the herbs, olive oil, and lime juice. Season to taste with salt. Serve the lima beans with the sauce and garnish with the remaining herbs and strips of lime zest.

Chicken scallops with pesto and green beans

Ingredients
- 8 chicken breast fillets, skin removed
- 10 oz (300 g) soft goat cheese
- 2 tbsp oil
- 8 tbsp pesto (Italian basil sauce, on the pasta sauce aisle in the supermarket)
- 1 3/4 lb (800 g) stringless green beans
- 2 tsp butter
- Salt and pepper

Equipment
- 1 small, sharp knife
- 1 large ovenproof dish
- 1 large saucepan
- 1 sieve

How long it will take
30 minutes preparation time
+ 15 minutes cooking time

Method
Preheat the oven to 400 °F (200 °C). Carefully cut along one side of each chicken breast to form a pocket (sometimes, chicken breast fillets already come in two pieces, in which case there is no need to create a pocket). Fill the pockets with the goat cheese. Pour the oil into the ovenproof dish and add the chicken scallops. Season with salt and pepper and spread a tablespoon of pesto over each scallop. Wash and dry the green beans, then top and tail each bean. A quicker way is to take a handful of beans and trim the ends with a knife. Bring a large saucepan of salted water to a boil. When the oven is hot, put the chicken dish in to cook for 15 minutes. When the saucepan of water has come to a rolling boil, add the beans and cook for 12 minutes, then drain and place in a serving dish with the butter, and combine, adding a little salt if necessary. Take the chicken out of the oven and you're ready to serve.

Green apple and kiwi fruit salad

Ingredients

· 1 lemon
· 4 tbsp superfine sugar
· 8 kiwi fruit
· 6 Granny Smith apples
· 8 mint leaves

Equipment

· 1 lemon squeezer
· 1 potato peeler

How long it will take

30 minutes preparation time
+ 2 hours chilling time

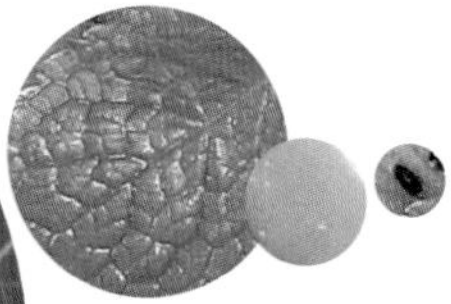

Method

Squeeze the lemon, then combine the juice with the sugar, stirring until dissolved. Peel and slice the kiwi fruit. Wash the apples, then cut into quarters. Remove the cores and cut into thin slices, leaving the skin on. In a large mixing bowl, combine the apples, kiwi fruit, and lemon juice. Allow to chill for at least 2 hours in the refrigerator, stirring occasionally. When ready to serve, wash and dry the mint leaves. Using scissors, cut into fine strips and scatter over the fruit salad. If you desire, you can leave a few leaves whole for decoration.

All pink dinner

or

how to see the world through rose-tinted glasses

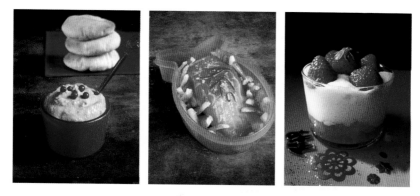

Homemade tara-masalata with pink peppercorns

Single side sautéed salmon and pink radish stir-fry

Tiramisu with straw-berries

Pink, it is said, is a girl's favorite color. It is also said that baby girls are born in a bed of roses. Pink is the color of sweet, soft, and pretty things:

- cotton candy
- Barbie doll dresses
- rose petals
- strawberry ice cream
- pink champagne
- Alpine strawberries ...

It's so pretty... a dinner fit for a princess." Antonia, who has something childlike about her

Organization

The evening before, you can ...
· Make the taramasalata.

A few hours before the meal, you can ...
· Prepare, but not cook, the radish.
· Make the French dressing.
· Make the tiramisu.

"La vie en rose, la vie en rose. It makes me want to sing like Edith Piaf." Joanna, making a ful- some musical tribute

"Every now and then, a dinner party just for the girls really does you good." Alice, who is a bit fed up with guys at the moment

"An effective remedy for the blues, this all pink dinner. And what's more, it's prettier than the little pills." Claudine, who isn't down in the dumps at all any more

Homemade taramasalata
with pink peppercorns

Ingredients

· About 1 1/4 lb (600 g) smoked cod roe
· 2 lemons
· 2 slices sandwich bread
· A little milk to soak the bread
· 3/4 cup (200 ml) oil
· 1/4 cooked beet (to produce the pink color)
· About 40 pink peppercorns
· Pita breads or blinis

Equipment

· 1 lemon squeezer
· 1 blender

How long it will take

20 minutes preparation time
+ 5 minutes to warm the pita breads

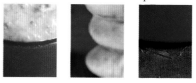

Method

Cut the cod roe into pieces. Squeeze one of the lemons. Remove the crusts from the bread, then soak the bread in the milk, and squeeze out using your hands. Put the cod roe, lemon juice, and bread in the blender, then blend in bursts, adding the oil gradually until the mixture is creamy and easy to spread. Cut the beet into pieces and add to the mixture in the blender a little at a time until it has attained the desired color. Cut the remaining lemon in two, then cut each half into four. Warm the blinis or pitas in an oven (about 5 minutes at 210 °F/100 °C in a traditional oven or 1 minute in a microwave oven). Sprinkle the taramasalata with the pink peppercorns and serve with the pita breads or blinis and the lemon segments.

Single side sautéed salmon and pink radish stir-fry

Ingredients

· 2 bunches pink radishes
· 9 tbsp hazelnut or olive oil
· 3 tbsp cider vinegar (or another fairly mild vinegar)
· 7 tbsp oil (for cooking)
· 8 skinless salmon steaks (you can ask your fish merchant to skin them)
· Salt

Equipment

· I potato peeler
· 2 skillets
· I large saucepan

How long it will take

30 minutes preparation time
+ 15 minutes cooking time

Method

Remove the tops (green leaves) from the radishes. Wash and dry the radishes. Remove strips of skin from four of the radishes using a potato peeler and set them aside for the garnish. Cut the remaining radishes in four lengthwise to make small sticks. Combine the hazelnut oil with the cider vinegar and some salt. Open the window and close the door: salmon produces a strong smell when cooking. Heat the skillets over a high heat. When hot, pour 2 tablespoons of cooking oil into each one. When the oil is hot, add the salmon fillets with the side where the skin was (the flat side) facing down. They will take about 8–10 minutes to cook. After 2 minutes, reduce to a moderate heat. The side of the salmon that is next to the base of the skillet will become very crisp, while the top surface will remain almost raw. To find out if the salmon is sufficiently cooked, touch the top surface with your finger. If it is still cold, it is not cooked enough; the salmon is cooked as soon as the top is properly warm. While cooking the salmon, put 3 tablespoons of cooking oil to heat over a moderate heat in the large saucepan. Add the radishes and sauté for about 5 minutes until they are slightly translucent but still crisp. Serve the salmon drizzled with the hazelnut oil dressing and garnished with the strips of radish skin, alongside the stir-fried radish sticks.

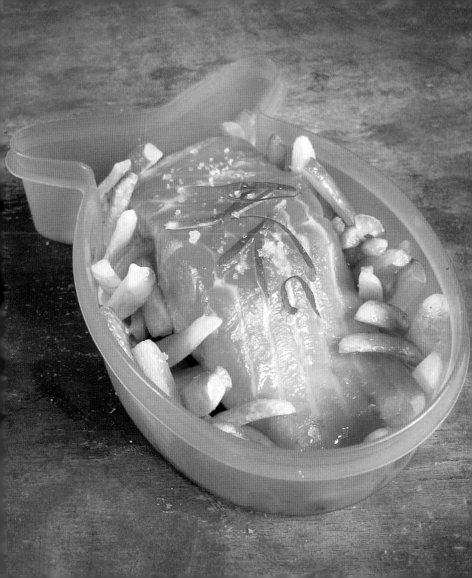

Tiramisu with strawberries

Ingredients

- 1 2/3 cups (250 g) strawberries
- 1 cup (250 g) mascarpone cheese (very creamy Italian cream cheese)
- 2 cups (500 g) plain whole milk yogurt
- Scant 1/2 cup sugar
- 6 egg whites
- A pinch of salt
- 32 pink champagne Reims cookies (use ladyfingers if not available)
- 2 cups (500 ml) strawberry nectar drink (or strawberry syrup diluted with a little water)

Equipment

- 1 electric beater to beat the egg whites into stiff peaks, or 1 hand beater (but it is quite hard work)
- 2 large mixing bowls
- 1 large dish or 8 bowls or ramekins

How long it will take

25 minutes preparation time

Method

Quickly wash the strawberries under running water and dry them immediately. Hull the strawberries (remove the leaves). In a large glass bowl, combine the mascarpone, yogurt, and sugar. Put the egg whites in a large mixing bowl with the salt and slowly start to beat, increasing the speed gradually. When they turn very white and quite firm (forming stiff peaks in the mixing bowl), fold them into the yogurt and mascarpone mixture, stirring gently. Put the pink champagne cookies or ladyfingers to soak in the strawberry nectar drink. When they have soaked it up, drain them (it doesn't matter too much if they break). Arrange them over the base of the dish or the ramekins. Spread the creamy cheese mixture over the cookies and, when ready to serve, top with the strawberries.

Fusion food dinner

or

how to go on your travels
without leaving the dining room

Cheesy polenta cake

*Coconut and chicken
curry with lime rice*

*Crispy date and
almond mille-feuilles*

It's trendy, cool, fashionable… you too. It wasn't long ago that fusion food made its appearance on our plates and it's not about to disappear. But what is it exactly? Fusion food is the term used to describe dishes that combine flavors, techniques, spices, or herbs from other parts of the world with products or recipes from home. Fusion food is not primarily about the quest for authentic food from abroad (often very complicated, or even totally unrealistic, to reproduce at home). But what it is about is a way of trying out "border free" cooking. It's about giving the imagination the freedom to blend, combine, and associate ingredients.

Organization

"The only thing I know about fusion food is that it's good." Robert, who doesn't like to ask himself questions when he's eating

The evening before, you can…

· Make the cheesy polenta cake, but save the browning for later.
· Cook the pastry triangles for the mille-feuilles.

A few hours before the meal, you can…

· Cook the rice. Just reheat it with a little butter and add the lime juice at the last minute.

"Fusion cookery harmoniously unites people at the dinner table." Marie, who appreciates the group dynamic

· Layer up the mille-feuilles with the dates, but save the hot sauce for later.

Just before your guests arrive, you can…

· Prepare the salad for the polenta cake.
· Cook the chicken strips, keeping them in the refrigerator once cooked.

Cheesy polenta cake

Ingredients

· 1/2 lb (250 g) instant polenta
· 4 cups (1 liter) milk
· 8 slices raclette or other melting cheese
· 16 slices cured meat
· 16 small gherkins
· About 6 cups (300 g) salad (such as baby spinach leaves)
· 4 tbsp vinegar
· 4 tbsp oil
· Salt and pepper

Equipment

· 1 large saucepan
· 2 loaf pans or 1 nonstick tart pan
· 1 pastry brush or 1 paper towel

How long it will take

30 minutes preparation time
+ 20 minutes cooking time
+ 1 hour setting time

Method

Prepare the polenta with the milk following the instructions on the package. If it seems too thick, add a little water or milk at the end of the cooking time. Season with salt and pepper. If necessary, remove the rind from the cheese. Transfer half the polenta mixture to the loaf pans or tart pan, arrange the cheese slices on top, then top with the remaining polenta. Place in the refrigerator for at least 1 hour to set. Cut the cured meat into strips and cut the gherkins into four lengthwise. Wash and dry the salad if necessary. Pour the vinegar into a bowl, add 3 tablespoons of oil, stirring constantly. When ready to serve, heat the broiler. Take the polenta out of the refrigerator, pour 1 tablespoon of oil on top and spread it all over the polenta using some paper towel or a pastry brush. When the broiler is hot, place the pan(s) under the broiler and wait until the surface becomes golden and crisp (it will take 3–5 minutes). Remove from the broiler and allow to cool for 5 minutes. Meanwhile, divide the salad, meat, and gherkins between the plates and drizzle with the French dressing. Cut the polenta cake into eight pieces and place atop the salad.

Coconut and chicken curry with lime rice

Ingredients

- 16 sprigs cilantro
- 2 handfuls peanuts
- 2 limes
- 8 skinless chicken breast fillets
- 3 tbsp oil
- 2 cups (400 g) long-grain rice (basmati)
- 3 1/3 cups (800 ml) coconut milk
- 1 tbsp curry powder
- Salt

Equipment

- 1 zester or potato peeler
- 1 lemon squeezer
- 1 large nonstick skillet
- 2 large saucepans or heatproof casserole dishes
- 1 sieve

How long it will take

30 minutes preparation time
+ 30 minutes cooking time

Method

Wash and dry the cilantro. Cut the leaves into fine strips using scissors or a knife. Chop the peanuts into small pieces or crush them with a rolling pin (if you have no rolling pin, use a bottle). Zest the limes or remove strips of zest using a potato peeler and cut them into fine shreds. Squeeze the limes. Cut the chicken breasts into 1/2 inch (1 cm) wide strips. Heat the skillet over a high heat, then add the oil. When the oil is hot, add the chicken. Season with salt and cook for about 3 minutes until browned on all sides. Cook the rice in a saucepan following the instructions on the package. Meanwhile, pour the coconut milk and curry powder into a large saucepan and bring to a boil. Add the chicken pieces and reduce the heat. Simmer for 5 minutes. Drain the rice and combine with the lime juice. Garnish with the lime zest. Serve the chicken with the rice, crushed peanuts, and the cilantro.

Crispy date and almond mille-feuilles

Ingredients

· 3 sheets brick pastry (very thin Tunisian pastry obtainable from specialty Asian markets; use phyllo pastry as an alternative)
· 2 tsp butter
· 80 soft, moist dates
· 1 cup (100 g) slivered almonds
· 16 tbsp honey
· 8 tbsp orange-flower water (available from gourmet markets)

Equipment

· 1 pastry brush or some paper towels
· 1 baking sheet
· 1 small saucepan
· 1 skillet

How long it will take

30 minutes preparation time
+ 15 minutes cooking time

Method

Preheat the oven to 300 °F (150 °C). Get out the sheets of brick pastry. They are separated by sheets of paper to prevent them from sticking to each other. Remove them very carefully, because they are fragile. Cut each sheet of pastry into six triangles (you will be using 16 in total). Place them on one of the pieces of paper that separated the pastry sheets. Melt the butter in a small saucepan over a low heat. Spread the melted butter over the pastry sheets using a pastry brush or paper towel. Bake in the oven for about 3 minutes until they are beautifully golden. Repeat the process with the remaining batches. Cut the dates in half and remove the pits. Arrange the dates over 16 pastry triangles. Place half the date triangles on plates. Heat a skillet over a high heat. Add the slivered almonds and sauté until golden. Sprinkle the almonds over the dates. When

ready to serve, heat the honey in a small saucepan together with the orange-flower water, stirring to combine. When the mixture comes to a boil, pour half of it over the eight pastry triangles on the plates, top with the remaining triangles, and pour over the remaining sauce. Serve immediately.

Dinner to go or
a picnic

or

pack-away portable menu

Chicken liver mousse
with raisins

Wheat tabbouleh

Mock banana crumble

This menu is suitable for two types of occasion.

1. For a traditional picnic, prepare everything in advance and, when the time comes to go to table, or rather, to "tablecloth," all you need do is combine the ingredients. That way, everything stays deliciously fresh and crisp. The distinction between appetizer and main course has no meaning here. It is up to you how to organize this meal which, by definition, is not very formal.

2. If friends invite you round for a meal and ask you to bring part or even all of the meal, all you need do is dip into the suggested dishes. They are all easy to transport in containers or boxes.

"To be honest, this chicken liver mousse is almost as good as foie gras."
Élisabeth, who is definitely going to do this recipe again

"I love picnics. Especially when you eat well."
Sébastien, honest and to the point

Organization

The evening before, you can…
· Make the chicken liver mousse.
· Make the wheat tabbouleh.

A few hours before the meal, you can…
· Make the banana cream for the crumble.
· Prepare the tabbouleh garnish.

"First the mobile phone, then portable music, and now here's the movable feast, it really is part of the trend toward 'consumption on the move.'"
Amélie, amateur sociologist

Chicken liver mousse with raisins

Ingredients

- 6 tbsp cognac or port (use water for children)
- 2/3 cup (100 g) raisins
- Scant 1 cup (200 g) butter
- 2 onions
- 2 tsp butter (for cooking)
- 1 lb 2 oz (500 g) chicken livers
- Salt and pepper
- Walnut bread and gherkins to serve

Equipment

- 1 saucepan
- 1 large skillet
- 1 blender
- 1 loaf pan
- plastic wrap

How long it will take

15 minutes preparation time
+ 15 minutes cooking time
+ 24 hours chilling time

Method

Heat the cognac or port in the saucepan. When hot, remove from the heat and add the raisins. Allow to soak. Cut the 1 cup (200 g) butter into small pieces. Peel, halve, and finely slice the onions. Heat the skillet over a moderate heat, melt the 2 teaspoons of butter, add the sliced onions, season with salt, and cook for 10 minutes until translucent. Add the chicken livers, season with salt, and cook for 5 minutes, stirring so that they cook on all sides. Season with pepper 1 minute before the end of the cooking time. Process the contents of the skillet in a blender, adding the pieces of butter gradually, to produce a smooth mixture. Drain the raisins. Line the loaf pan with plastic wrap. Spoon in a third of the mousse mixture and sprinkle with the raisins. Add another third of the mousse mixture, sprinkle with the remaining raisins, and top with the remaining mousse mixture. Cover with plastic wrap and refrigerate for at least 24 hours. When ready to eat, turn the mousse out and serve with walnut bread and gherkins.

Wheat tabbouleh

Ingredients

· 2 lemons
· 6 cups (1 kg) durum wheat (such as Ebly Tender Wheat) or bulghur
· 8 tbsp olive oil
· 4 tomatoes
· 2 green bell peppers
· 1 cucumber
· 4 scallions or 2 ordinary onions
· 16 mint leaves
· Salt

Equipment

· 1 lemon squeezer
· 1 large saucepan
· 1 potato peeler

How long it will take

30 minutes preparation time
+ 10 minutes cooking time

Method

Squeeze the lemons. Cook the wheat following the instructions on the package, then drain. Pour the olive oil and lemon juice over the wheat. Combine and allow to cool. Check the seasoning, adding a little salt if necessary. Wash and dry the tomatoes and bell peppers. Cut the tomatoes into quarters and remove the seeds and pulp. Cut the flesh into small pieces. Cut the bell peppers into quarters and remove the seeds and white membranes with a knife. Cut the flesh into small pieces. Using a potato peeler, peel the cucumber, then cut in half lengthwise. Scoop out the seeds with a tablespoon and discard, then cut the flesh into small pieces. Peel the scallions by trimming the ends and removing the top layer of skin. Cut them in half, lay them flat side down, and slice finely, then cut again at right angles to make small dice. Wash and dry the mint leaves. Using a knife or scissors, cut them into thin strips. When ready to serve, combine the vegetables with the wheat and sprinkle with the mint.

146

Mock banana crumble

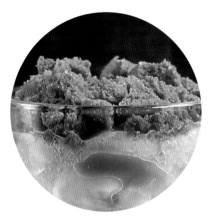

Ingredients

- 6 bananas
- 1 lemon
- 8 tbsp superfine sugar
- 3 1/3 cups (800 g) fromage blanc or mascarpone
- 8 slices gingerbread

Equipment

- 1 lemon squeezer

How long it will take

10 minutes preparation time

Method

Peel four of the bananas. Squeeze the lemon. Using a fork, mash the bananas together with the sugar and lemon juice. When ready to serve, peel the remaining bananas. Spoon the fromage blanc or mascarpone into glasses or bowls, followed by the mashed banana, then add the banana slices. To finish, crumble a slice of gingerbread over each glass or bowl.

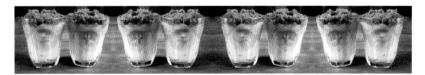

Sweet and sour dinner

or

how to bring together contrasting tastes

Oven-roasted figs with soft goat cheese

Tagine of lamb with citrus fruit and honey

Peach and salted butter crumble

Nobody knows whether cave men had the brilliant idea of eating their mammoth steaks with the berries they gathered, but one thing that is certain is that there is nothing new about sweet and sour cookery. The Romans cooked with honey (at least, that is what they say in Asterix); in the Middle Ages, they ate meat with raisin and almond sauces; and duck à l'orange or roast pork with apple sauce are part of our classical cookery heritage.

Why is it good? Combining flavors that are in some way opposites highlights them to mutual beneficial effect. Salt is what is called a flavor enhancer, in other words it brings out the flavors of foods. That is why, in many cake recipes, a pinch of salt will feature in the list of ingredients. You can take things a step further still by making all your pastry with salted butter. Nobody will really notice it, but your desserts will have that little extra something that makes all the difference.

Organization

The evening before, you can...
· Make the crumble mixture, wrapping it in plastic wrap and storing it in the refrigerator overnight.

A few hours before the meal, you can...
· Prepare the figs; then all you will have to do is pop them in the oven.
· Prepare the lamb; then all you will have to do is reheat it gently.
· Prepare the crumble; then all you will have to do is pop it in the oven.

"I love being surprised when I'm invited to dinner." Aurélie, who can come again

Oven-roasted figs with soft goat cheese

Ingredients

· 24 fresh figs
· 4 cartons of Chavignol or 1/2 lb (225 g) other semifirm goat cheese
· 8 tsp honey
· 8 tbsp olive oil
· 3 tbsp vinegar
· 4 cups (200 g) corn salad
· Salt and pepper

Equipment

· 1 large ovenproof dish

How long it will take

10 minutes preparation time
+ 15 minutes cooking time

Method

Preheat the oven to 350 °F (180 °C). Wash and dry the figs, then split them from top to bottom, leaving the two halves attached at the base. Sprinkle the insides of the figs with salt and pepper. Divide the cheese into 24 pieces and insert one piece into each fig. Season with salt and pepper. Place the figs in an ovenproof dish and drizzle a little honey over. Bake for 10 minutes, then place under a broiler and cook for an additional 3–5 minutes, until the cheese turns a pale golden color. While the figs are cooking, combine the olive oil and vinegar. Wash and dry the salad if necessary. Toss the salad with the oil and vinegar dressing. Arrange the salad on plates, top with three figs per plate, and serve.

Tagine of lamb with citrus fruit and honey

Ingredients

- 3 lb 5 oz (1.5 kg) boneless lamb
- 4 oranges
- 2 grapefruit
- 4 onions
- 6 tbsp oil
- 8 tbsp honey
- 1 tbsp ground cinnamon
- 1 tbsp paprika
- 2 tbsp coriander seeds
- 2 3/4 cups (500 g) couscous
- Salt
- Cinnamon sticks (optional garnish)

Equipment

- 1 large saucepan with lid
- 1 heatproof casserole dish or 1 large saucepan
- 1 nonstick skillet
- 1 zester or 1 potato peeler
- 1 lemon squeezer

How long it will take

15 minutes preparation time
+ 1 hour 40 minutes cooking time

Method

Cut the lamb into cubes measuring about 1 1/2 inches (4 cm) square. Wash and dry the oranges. Remove the orange zest using a zester or, alternatively, remove strips of zest using a potato peeler and then cut them into fine shreds. Squeeze the oranges and grapefruit. Peel the onions, cutting and removing the dry skin. Then cut them in half, place each half flat side down and slice finely. Warm 2 tablespoons of oil in the casserole dish over a moderate heat. Add the onions and cook for about 10 minutes. They should become soft and transparent, without browning. Heat the skillet over a high heat. When it is hot, add 2 tablespoons of oil. When the oil is very hot, add the cubed lamb, season with salt, and brown all over. If the lamb won't all fit into the skillet, brown it in batches, adding more oil if necessary.

When the onions are cooked, transfer the browned lamb to the casserole dish. Add the orange and grapefruit juice, honey, ground cinnamon, paprika, and coriander seeds. If necessary add a little water so that the meat is just covered with liquid. Add a little salt and cover. Allow to cook over a low heat for 1 1/2 hours, taking a look from time to time and adding a little water if there is not enough juice. At the end of the cooking time, the juice should be syrupy. If it is not, remove the meat from the casserole and boil the sauce until it thickens. Meanwhile, cook the couscous following the instructions on the package so that it is cooked at the same time as the lamb. Serve the lamb garnished with the strips of orange zest and the cinnamon sticks, if using.

Peach and salted butter crumble

Ingredients

· 12 peaches
· 2/3 cup (150 g) salted butter
· 1 1/4 cups (150 g) flour
· 2/3 cup (150 g) raw brown sugar
· 2/3 cup (100 g) ground almonds

Equipment

· 1 baking dish
· 1 potato peeler

How long it will take

30 minutes preparation time
+ 30 minutes cooking time

Method

Preheat the oven to 350 °F (180 °C). Cut the peaches into quarters and remove the pits. Peel the quarters and cut into small pieces, then place in the baking dish. Cut the butter into small pieces. Put the butter, flour, sugar, and ground almonds in a bowl. Using the fingertips, blend the pieces of butter into the flour until they are all incorporated and the mixture resembles bread crumbs. Spread this mixture over the fruit to form a crust. When the oven has reached the correct temperature, put the dish in the oven and bake for about 30 minutes. The crust should then be beautifully golden. Remember to check the oven from time to time to ensure that the crumble is not browning too much. If it is, reduce the temperature to 300 °F (150 °C) and continue cooking. On the other hand, if it is not already golden after 20 minutes, increase the temperature to 400 °F (200 °C). Take the dish out of the oven and allow to cool for 5 minutes before serving.

Recipe index by appetizer / main course / dessert

Appetizers

Main courses

- Crispy eggplant with feta cheese 106
- Crispy pork spareribs, whole corn 58
- Duck and turnip carpaccio 98
- Duck breasts with foie gras and morels 66
- Meat and potato pie 90
- Roast beef and gnocchi with Gorgonzola cream sauce 114
- Roast pork with gingerbread cream sauce and apple 34
- Salmon, leek, and orange parcels 74
- Shredded southern chicken 18
- Single side sautéed salmon and pink radish stir-fry 130
- Tagine of lamb with citrus fruit and honey 154
- Tuna in a tapenade crust with Parmesan pasta 50
- Wheat tabbouleh 146

Desserts

- Brioche club sandwiches 60
- Chocolate and candied orange tart 68
- Chocolate and ginger soup with litchis 84
- Coconut tartlets with sautéed mango 108
- Cream cheese tart 116
- Cream cheese with maple syrup and pecan nuts 52
- Crispy date and almond mille-feuilles 140
- Green apple and kiwi fruit salad 124
- Green apple mousse 28
- Mock banana crumble 148
- Crêpe moneybags with Nutella mousse 76
- Peach and salted butter crumble 156
- Pears poached in wine, star anise, and crème de cassis 36
- Readymade sweet pastry tartlets 44
- Strawberry and melon tartare with port 100
- Sumptuous chocolate and apricot cake 20
- Tiramisu with strawberries 132

How the book came about

nicole.seeman@laposte.net

I always write cookbooks for the people around me (the books have very long titles). The first, *The cookbook for guys who want to impress girls, but have little equipment and even less experience*, was intended for those of my male friends who were not really very acquainted with their ovens. The second, *The cookbook for girls who haven't learned much from their mothers*, was written at the request of my girl friends who were not very experienced in the culinary arts.

I am not a professional cook, just an enthusiastic amateur who understands the questions you ask yourself when you don't have any experience of cooking, because I ask them myself in just the same way.

In this book, I have chosen to deal with another subject from everyday life: the dinner party at home for eight people. I have cooked a lot of them. Some good ones, some not so good, some that, frankly, were failures. Initially, I treated each dinner party like a final in the Olympic Games, and sometimes I didn't deserve even a chocolate medal. What I ended up understanding was that it doesn't really matter, because it's not what's on your plate that makes for a successful dinner party. Since then, I've become cooler and I enjoy the evenings more. I even manage to join in the conversation without thinking about the dish that I'm going to serve next. And when I don't have the time to do everything, so what! As they say, it's the thought that counts and my intentions are always good...

Nicole Seeman